It Isn't Fair!

IT ISN'T FAIR!

Siblings of Children with Disabilities

Edited by
STANLEY D. KLEIN
and
MAXWELL J. SCHLEIFER

An Exceptional Parent Press Publication

BERGIN & GARVEY
Westport, Connecticut • London

Library of Congress Cataloging-in-Publication Data

It isn't fair! : siblings of children with disabilities / edited by
   Stanley D. Klein and Maxwell J. Schleifer.
       p.   cm.
     "An Exceptional Parent Press publication."
     Includes bibliographical references and index.
     ISBN 0–89789–332–8 (hc : alk. paper).—ISBN 0–89789–333–6 (pbk.
  : alk paper)
     1. Handicapped children—United States—Family relationships.
     2. Brothers and sisters—United States.   I. Klein, Stanley D.
     II. Schleifer, Maxwell J. (Maxwell Joseph).
     HV888.5.I7   1993
     362.4′043′083—dc20   92–38707

British Library Cataloguing in Publication Data is available.

Library of Congress Catalog Card Number: 92–38707
ISBN: 0–89789–332–8 (hc); 0–89789–333–6 (pb)

First published in 1993

Bergin & Garvey, 88 Post Road West, Westport, CT 06881
An imprint of Greenwood Publishing Group, Inc.

Printed in the United States of America

∞™

The paper used in this book complies with the
Permanent Paper Standard issued by the National
Information Standards Organization (Z39.48–1984).

10 9 8 7 6 5 4 3 2 1

Dedicated to Esther Lederer (Ann Landers)

Without the continued support and encouragement of this world famous columnist, thousands of parents would never have heard of *Exceptional Parent* magazine. And, *Exceptional Parent* magazine would not have survived.

Contents

Acknowledgments

For over twenty years *Exceptional Parent* magazine has been a major preoccupation of our lives. Many wonderful people have helped in the development of *Exceptional Parent*. Talented parents and people with disabilities have played major roles as have many professionals and the dedicated, hard working, and underpaid *Exceptional Parent* staff members.

Juliet Lovejoy contributed a great deal to creating this book. As an editorial intern, she did many thankless chores in addition to helping create the introductory material to each section.

John Harney has been very helpful with his advice and kind patience.

Introduction

In 1972 *Exceptional Parent* magazine first published an interview with four college students, each of whom had a sibling with a disability. Families raising a child with a disability at home at that time did so in the context of very limited educational or therapeutic services for the child and little or no community support. Accordingly, each college student had grown up in a family setting where parents and other family members provided most of the care needed by the child. They did so in communities that were years away from being sensitized to current concepts of inclusion and community participation of children and adults with disabilities.

In those days, when a child with a noticeable disability was born, parents were often advised to institutionalize the baby. Professionals believed the parents would be assuming a terrible burden by taking the child home and that the rest of the family, and especially the other children, would suffer. Even though the professional literature was beginning to discuss positive as well as negative outcomes for family members when a child with a disability was raised at home, many professionals continued to believe it would be harmful to the family. Describing those times in "Forgotten Children," Meyer Schreiber writes: "The simple fact is that our concept of the family does not include a place for the family with a child with a disability. . . . Only now is the disabled child coming to be perceived as a human being with the same basic needs for love, acceptance and belonging as other children."

Despite the vast changes of the past two decades for children with disabilities and their parents and siblings, most of the issues discussed by the four college students in 1972 continue to be relevant to family life today. They are issues that deal with essential relationships between sisters and brothers, and children and parents. Although certain issues can have particular poignancy when one child has a disability or serious health problem, the issues of fairness, parental expectations, rewards and punishments, caretaking responsibilities, and negative feelings between siblings are common to all developing families. One issue, the role of straightforward communication within families, is a motivating factor for this book as well as for *Exceptional Parent* magazine's continuing attention to sisters and brothers and family relationships.

The participants' interview with *Exceptional Parent* was the first time they had ever discussed their sibling relationships with peers who had similar life experiences. Subsequently, the publication of the interview and a gradually growing professional literature stimulated similar group discussions. Today, the value of siblings of children with disabilities or special health care needs talking with one another, with parents, and with professionals is widely acknowledged.

STRUCTURE

The book is divided into five parts. In Part I, the interview with the college students is followed by an article by Meyer Schreiber, one of the first professionals to write and speak about the needs of siblings. In Part II, there are eight articles by parents and one by a team of professionals. In Part III, there are seven articles written by siblings reflecting on their experiences. A series of case studies highlighting sibling relationships follows in Part IV. The book concludes with Part V and a series of brief articles written by children, first published in *Exceptional Parent*'s regular feature, "Family Album."

Each article in this book was published in *Exceptional Parent* from 1972 to 1992. These two decades saw dramatic changes in community attitudes about people with disabilities and their families and in opportunities for children and adults with disabilities to participate in everyday community life. These changes have meant that families can look outside themselves for resources. There is now greater community understanding and appreciation of parenting within a family that includes a child with special needs. Still, parents' desires to meet the needs of all their children in constructive ways continue, as do those common everyday interactions between sisters and brothers about which parents wish they had more information, patience, and energy.

From this collection, it is clear that children, just like their parents, need accurate information about a sibling's disability presented with compassion and understanding. It is also clear that siblings benefit from talking with people like themselves who are coping with similar life experiences. Overall, this reminds us, as stated at the end of the sibling interview: "We can learn and relearn by our willingness to listen to other human beings. . . . As parents and professionals we need to be reminded by the inner strength of our fellow humans. We need to be reminded that a disabled child has siblings and parents and relatives and neighbors, each one can learn from the other."

PART I

Siblings Begin to Talk Together

Although the four young women and men did not know each other before they were interviewed for "Brother to Sister, Sister to Brother," they readily got into a poignant discussion despite the unusual circumstances of a television studio and the knowledge that every word was being recorded.

Each person's situation is different: Richard's younger brother has a noticeable physical disability and a hearing impairment; Tracy's older brother is mentally retarded as a result of brain damage and he walks with a limp; Gary's younger brother is autistic; Diane's younger sister is severely retarded and does not walk or talk. (Prior to publication, all identifying names and locations were changed.)

During the interview, the participants speak of many experiences: early memories of trips to therapies and hospitals, observing teasing of a brother or sister, trying to protect a sibling, personal embarrassment and fury, taking advantage of a sibling, guilty feelings, resenting extra chores, jealousy, parents talking or not talking about the sibling's disability, and the impact of their brother or sister on their social lives as teenagers as well as their current relationships. They also discuss their concerns about the future. Similar experiences are described by sisters and brothers in Part III.

At the end of the interview, each person spoke about how much she or he learned from the experiences—negative and positive—in their families. They also spoke about the value of talking to one another. The publication of this discussion in *Exceptional Parent* stimulated many similar discussions in local communities.

One of the first conferences held after the publication of "Brother to Sister, Sister to Brother," took place in Providence, Rhode Island in 1974 under the sponsorship of the Rhode Island Easter Seals Society. We adapted Meyer Schreiber's keynote address at that conference for the article "Forgotten Children." In it, Schreiber, a social worker, described early 1970s life within the wider society of families with a disabled child. He noted the power of the myth that said "a seriously disabled child cannot live at home" and how the burden of changing this myth and thereby changing society was carried by parents themselves. He urged parents "to provide help, direction, understanding and explanation to sisters and brothers."

At the same conference, Stanley D. Klein, one of the editors who moderated the *Exceptional Parent* interview, again moderated a panel discussion that included siblings. Excerpts of the comments of the sibling speakers at the conference are in italics in "Forgotten Children."

Schreiber also presented the issues that typically arise as children develop—issues that are addressed in "Brother to Sister, Sister to Brother" and are addressed by parents and siblings in the articles that follow. As preschoolers and elementary school aged children learn about the world around them, they begin to notice differences and need information. They also become aware of the importance of attention from adults—who gets it and why. As a result, they are likely to feel hostile or jealous when their sister or brother who is disabled gets extra attention. Those feelings need to be acknowledged with support and understanding.

For teenagers with a growing social world, the opinions of peers, including opinions about their sibling with a disability, become extremely important and again they will need information, but at a different level. Later, as young adults, siblings again need information and understanding—for their concerns about genetics and their worries about the possible caretaking responsibilities in the years to come.

Brother to Sister,
Sister to Brother

Four college students were invited by Dr. Stanley Klein, Editor of *Exceptional Parent*, to meet together to talk about their experiences as the brother or sister of a person with a disability.

None of the participants knew each other before the discussion. Each one had some contact with Dr. Klein or another member of *Exceptional Parent* staff. The interview lasted for two hours. It has been edited, and identifying names and locations have been changed.

Richard: I never thought of thinking about my relationship to my brother until I mentioned it to Dr. Klein in a different context and he presented the idea of this discussion to me. Then I *did* start thinking about it to an extent. But this morning, I have felt myself really holding down those thoughts until we really get into it. I am kind of anxious. I wonder what the hell is going to come out because I really have not discussed this with anyone.

Gary: I think that this sort of thing is beneficial because in the last hundred years, people's problems used to be locked up in closets, put away, shut off from the rest of society. Now society as a whole is taking a look at it and saying maybe it's not their fault.

Tracy: I think we are always being put in the position of defending our siblings. I think it is important to talk them up as to their good points, as well as their disabilities. When you are defending, you really cannot get into that as much.

Dr. K.: Can you describe the "sibling" that we are talking about?

Richard: My brother is twenty-one, I am older, and his name is Jim. I suppose you want to know the nature of the disability. He was born with four fingers on one hand and the elbow joint is somehow twisted, so where we would have our arm, his is twisted around. The other arm is about up to here [indicating his elbow] and there are two fingers there. It is difficult to explain.

When he was two years old he got the mumps which impaired his hearing quite a bit. So he is 90% deaf in one ear and stone deaf in the other ear. Because of that he has gone to special schools. When he went to a private school for the deaf, it was a trying kind of thing because most of the other kids who went to that school looked fine physically. Their only problem was with hearing. But my brother was just a little bit different.

He never did go to public school. He went from there to some other private school. Then he went to another school for the deaf away from home, which was really a very good experience for him because there the instructors were younger and much more enlightened.

Diane: Is he able to speak?

Richard: Yes, he speaks fairly well. Of course you really recognize the hearing problem because the way he says things truly reflects how he hears them. Sometimes I do not know if it is because certain tones do not come in, or what, but like only a part of a word might come out.

His mental ability seems to me to be quite adequate, all things considered. He has been through school and done OK as far as academics are concerned.

Diane: Is he still in school now?

Richard: No; now he is working. At that school for the deaf they taught him printing which he enjoyed quite a bit. He is now working for the state tourist agency. He runs a printing press over there.

Diane: Is he living at home?

Richard: Yes, he is living at home and he is thinking of how the hell he can move out. He wants to get some kind of independence.

Tracy: My brother is twenty-four and his name is Mark. He is four years older than me. He was born with a blood clot in his brain as a result of a forceps delivery. It resulted in brain damage to the left side of his brain which, as you probably know, affects the right-hand side of his body. I guess up to the point when he was fourteen years old, he had a series of operations: lengthening tendons in his legs, and eye operations because his eyes were crossed. The result of all the operations was really good cosmetically, because now you would not know by looking at him that he had brain damage, except for a slight limp. But his mental ability was pretty severely impaired. He has a lot of trouble with conceptual kinds of things. He cannot understand concepts and images, things like that, but he speaks well and he has a great sense of humor. And he has a really good auditory memory so he sounds like everybody else.

When he was about nineteen, my parents took him to the Philadelphia Institute for Human Potential. I do not know if you have heard about this. A lot of mentally retarded kids go through this kind of program. They creep and they crawl and do all kinds of exercises. It really helped him. He has always gone through public schools, he went to college, he went to Plano University, in Texas, which is for exceptional children, for two years. Then he went to business college for two years. Now he is in the city living with my parents, but Mom is trying to get him to learn how to cook and be able to live on his own. So he is doing pretty well considering . . .

Gary: I have a brother seven years of age who is autistic. From a practical standpoint, what it comes down to is he relates to objects rather than people. As a very young child, he would identify with radios and music; this is what would soothe him. Because he identifies with objects, his developmental growth is way behind. This is going to hurt him, I think, in the future. His name is Paul.

I do not think he is going to be able to follow the educational pattern of normal children because he does not relate to them as of now. It is going to be interesting to see what will happen.

Diane: Is he enrolled in any sort of program?

Gary: He is at a private day school for children with any kind of special problems. Outside of the fact that he does not relate to people, he is a happy boy. We try to keep him happy and being around the house, I see him every day and play with him and try to make him smile—as long as he is happy.

Diane: My sister's name is Cathy. She is twenty-one, two years younger than me. She is severely retarded. Her brain damage was a result of rubella. She does not walk and she does not talk. Her mental capacity, the doctors have said, is supposedly less than one year. Presently she is institutionalized in a state hospital. She was at home for seventeen years. She is a very happy child and my parents see her about once a week, or once every two weeks, and I see her perhaps once a month, or once every two months.

I find the older I get, the more difficult the visits become for some reason. I am not really sure why. But she is a really delightful child. She needs custodial care; really all she needs is love and attention. She has to be fed, of course, and bathed. She was never enrolled in any sort of special program because the prognosis was that she would never really improve.

She has improved physically somewhat, but she has not improved mentally. So she is at just about the same stage she was when she was six or seven as she is now at twenty-one.

Dr. K.: You mentioned things being different as you see them now. What are some of the early memories that you all have when you first noticed something about your sisters or brothers?

Diane: Because Cathy and I are only two years apart, I could never remember life without her, so that her sort of being different, I do not know, I guess it came very gradually.

Of course I noticed as I got older that she was indeed very different. She developed physically extremely slowly, so she was almost a perpetual infant. She was always referred to in the home as "the baby"; in fact, she still is. I can remember my mother saying that Cathy is sick, and we just have to give her very good care and that she probably will never be really well. It was just one of those things. It was never explained to me at any one time. I can never remember anything like that. It was a very gradual thing.

Tracy: First of all I can remember it being great fun as a kid, because he always had wheelchairs and crutches and all kinds of things that were just great fun to play with. But I never realized there was anything wrong with him, until other kids made fun of him. Then I started to realize he was different. Because when you play with someone you are that close to, you do not realize anything. Just like little kids not recognizing racial differences, I think. My parents strove so hard to make him seem normal that they never sat down with me and said, "Well look, Mark has certain disabilities that you have to recognize or help him with." They asked me to help him, but they did not say that he was sick or abnormal in any way.

Richard: I just thought of it in another way. I can remember quite sometime ago when we used to live on a farm. I remember playing with Jim in a barn, someplace. Just trying to put myself back into that, I cannot remember at all thinking, at that time, that there was anything different about him at all although it was very obvious, very clear, to see.

All of a sudden we started going into the hospital with him. Once a week, my mother and myself in the waiting room for hours and hours and hours. It was just incredible. Even then, I was always looking around at other people. I remember a big fat lady with a little kid that was just, I do not remember now, but I can just remember him as being a mess. I must have said to myself at that time, the kid is a mess and just marvelling over it. But here was my brother, and I never really noticed him.

Then one time when the doctors took him in, about seven doctors walked in the room with him. Then it just dawned on me, "What the hell are they doing in there?" They handed my mother what turned out to be an x-ray. I did not realize that it was of my own brother and it was an x-ray. It was an x-ray of his short arm and I looked at it and I said, "Ma, do you see that, that is somebody's foot." I said, "That is a foot and one part of it goes down like this and the other part goes up like this." And just at the last minute that I said that, it just dawned on me.

That was the thing that really slammed it home to me that that was really my brother. After that, one of the doctors suggested that I come in the room while they were examining him. Seeing the examination really elaborated on my realization. They would do these tests to see if he had any kind of muscular control in his two fingers. That was my realization.

Gary: With Paul, as he was growing up, there were a few differences. For instance, he would be put in a sitting position, and he would sit and draw his legs up to him. He never learned to crawl. He would leave his legs on the floor, draw his body up, and scoot around the floor this way. This was the first real sign outside of the fact that he was slow developing. He did not talk for a long time, he was two, or two and a half, and then he did not say much at all: a few lines, a few sentences. In the beginning stages, Mom and Dad used to console each other by saying he is going to outgrow this, he is slow in developing, that's all and, of course, that has not been the case.

He has improved lately. He does speak now. He wants certain definite things and he knows what he wants and keeps repeating. He will take you and what you say and will work it around to get what he wants. So he is quite clever in that way.

Dr. K.: When did you first think about how he was different?

Gary: Probably when he was around three or four, when it kept up. He used to sit in front of the record player, this is one of the ways he used to identify with objects, and just listen to music. It is sort of good in a way that he does not identify with people, if he is going to have a disability. He will get on the bus to go to school, or whatever, and the bus driver will yell at him to "sit down" and he does not listen to him, he just keeps on walking down the aisle until he finds a seat for himself, and then he climbs in. It does not bother him, so that is good. As long as he is happy, *that* is the most essential thing. And to correct the problem, if possible.

Dr. K.: You mentioned, Tracy, the issue of teasing, that was your first confrontation.

Tracy: I do not know what your experiences were because your sister was at home and your brother has been in a special school so you probably never went to school with him. I was able to see the interactions between the other kids and my brother. When I began junior high as a seventh grader, my brother was a ninth grader. Seventh graders, like me, were not known on the bus, and I heard some guy talking in the back about Mark and how stupid he was, and you could make him do anything and he is so gullible, and all this kind of stuff. I walked back to the kid and slugged him in the face. I was getting really annoyed and he could not understand what was happening.

I always felt that I had to protect him from someone, from teasing, from fights, and any other kids trying to put things over on kids who are at a disadvantage to them. If you love somebody you cannot help but get emotionally involved in that.

Richard: I remember one day standing up in front of the house. I must have been in about the sixth grade or so. One of my friends had just related an incident to me about how some other kids were picking on my brother and how he felt very sorry and all this stuff. Then he turned to me and said, "By the way, what *did* happen to your brother?" Looking back now, I can say well, I should have explained to him. But I just kind of got raging and I said, "Don't ask me that and the first person who asks me that after this, I am going to punch him in the face!" That was all there was to it, and I felt kind of strange. I questioned my sense of protectiveness of him and I wonder if it was not just really a denial of my own lack of understanding.

Tracy: Why can't anybody explain it. Say, "Listen, you have got to understand there is a problem here and you have to help him," but we cannot do that for some reason.

Richard: Something else happened, which I just remembered the other day, that shows me that maybe I have not progressed all that much. This past summer I worked at a playground. One day a bunch of kids and I were playing. Everybody stands in a circle and throws a ball to one another. And all of a sudden these little kids started dropping away from the circle. I was playing with them, so I did not really pay much attention to why some kids were dropping out. It was just slowly getting more and more quiet and I turned around: my brother was standing there. Of course, this is summertime, he has short sleeves on and these kids, even now I am tempted to say these little creeps, it really upset me—they made a circle around my brother, just made a circle around him and started looking at him and I just did not know what to do. On the one hand I felt like saying, and it upsets me now to think that I would say what I wanted to say, "Jim, hurry up and get out of here." Even now that I say it, it is totally disgusting and at the same time I wanted to say to all those little kids, "If you don't move now I am going to throw you all over the fence." Even now I have not resolved it—more than anything else, it shows me that I have not really come to terms with the whole thing. Furthermore, it gives me some appreciation for what my brother has to go through. He has to go every place.

Gary: I think that being in the position that we are, all having brothers and sisters, we can see it and therefore we can understand. When you have all these other little children or whomever, including grown adults, and they do not come in contact with it like we do, they do not understand it. So it is natural for them to stare to become familiar with this, like the time they were staring at your brother. Once they do become familiar with the idea, and they know who your brother is, then this will cease. I think the major problem is getting people to understand. People with special problems are just that; they are not to be pitied or scorned. In the case of your brother he can go out, he can get a job even with his disability.

Richard: Sometimes I wonder how he can do that.

Diane: I wonder if some people really want to understand. I say that on the basis of many of my experiences with Cathy. As I was growing older, I would bring my friends into the home. Because she was very retarded, she was never subjected to teasing and ridicule because she was never out in the neighborhood or around the school playing with the children. The only people she saw were our own friends. But a lot of friends that I brought home who did not know Cathy very well always wanted to know, "Why?" Why don't you put her away? Why don't you institutionalize her? We don't understand, she is such a burden, why are you keeping her at home? She is so much trouble for your mother, she is trouble for you, your family cannot go anywhere. They never understood that having her home was worth it all.

Tracy: When did your parents make the decision finally to institutionalize her?

Diane: Well, because both of my parents had to go to work. Of course, we were getting older and we were all in school and there was no one to stay home with her all day. She was getting bigger physically, too. She was much more difficult to carry and to handle, really.

Dr. K.: Did you experience the same kinds of feelings that Richard and Tracy are describing? That is, feeling embarrassed and feeling very furious all at the same time about other kids but also feeling something toward your brother or sister too.

Gary: No, not really. Something special, yes. Something toward them, the way other people do, no. The three little girls next door often play with Paul and with Stephen who is five, two years younger than Paul. Of course, they play with Stephen a little bit more. They used to come up to me and ask me about Paul and I would just tell them he is different. And they would accept that, so once you get over the initial hurdle . . .

Diane: I can remember being embarrassed about Cathy because she is really, I guess, quite upsetting to see for the first time. My family traveled a great deal. My father was in the service, so we frequently had to move to some new state or city. We traveled by bus, we traveled by plane, and ship; and, of course, Cathy was always with us. I can remember in a bus terminal we had to spread a blanket on the floor so Cathy could crawl around and get a little bit of exercise. A crowd gathered and I hated the people so much. I was just terribly embarrassed and I wanted to hide Cathy and I wanted to protect her from these people who were glaring, although she certainly did not know what was going on.

Tracy: I had an experience in high school. Mark had seizures, convulsive seizures, I guess what most people would think was an epileptic fit. When he started the Philadelphia program the activity started something in his brain and he began having seizures again even though he had not had them for many years. He had a seizure in class one day. The nurse could not keep Mark's medication in her office, so I carried it with me. She called me and the first thing she said to me so proudly was, "I got all the kids out of the room because it was so disgusting and they should not have to see that thing." And here he was, lying in the room alone, blue in the face, and she was so proud, because she had protected all the other kids while he was gagging. I never got over that.

Gary: Do you people feel that your brothers and sisters are as responsive, worried about it as we are?

Tracy: Mark denies it, but I really wonder . . .

Gary: Not like in what you think their inner thoughts might be, but in the way they actually express themselves, their actions, and everything. Are they as perturbed as we are, as worried about somebody else looking at them? In my case my little brother has his own built-in immunities and this is why I am asking.

Tracy: Mark kind of does not like anybody to know anything is wrong with him. I think it is just recently, when he started having seizures again in his adult life, that he realized there was something wrong with him.

Now he has slight little seizures, where his mouth will kind of droop, and sometimes he will drool and get bloodshot eyes, and then it will go in a second. He is really embarrassed if anybody sees him having it and he denies that anything is wrong with him if you ask. He knows but will not admit it. Maybe that is a result of our having made him deny his disability.

Diane: No, Cathy is so retarded that she is really not aware of other people's responses to her condition. She is certainly aware of love and attention, she likes music, different things. In fact through the years I have done a lot of thinking about how severe her condition is. I have known people who have had mongoloid children, for example, and children who are only mildly retarded and I have almost been sort of thankful, really, because she does not know and she is not subjected to any of the teasing, to any of the ridicule.

Her life is not hard as long as she has love and care and plenty to eat, she is very happy. She has a delightful disposition, she is always smiling; she is always laughing. I have sort of felt that I am glad she is this way, it sort of protects her, it shields her from the pains of the world.

Gary: It is an unfortunate fact, but it does make us realize how lucky we are.

Richard: My brother just seems like he has stopped worrying about it. Last week he and a friend of his went to Puerto Rico for the weekend. You can see little things in his behavior sometimes that show that he is conscious of it . . . sometimes he does not like to wear a short sleeved shirt, things like that. But I do not know. I think it is really fantastic development, or adaptation, but it is as if he were saying, well this is how I am and I make my adaptation as best I can and I live.

Tracy: And he does.

Dr. K.: In a way it is harder for you than for him.

Richard: That is right. One thing I feel guilty about is the fact that there was no reason for me to play "games" on my brother when he was five. We lived in a house where there was a wall that had a doorway on either side. It was just like there was one wall just there, with both ends open. I used to trick my brother into thinking that I could see through the wall and he could not. He honestly believed that, and now I can picture myself doing that stuff again. I am probably wrong; I am sure I am wrong. I feel kind of guilty for having done that kind of stuff. I took advantage of him and I really should not have.

Diane: I have an awful lot of feelings like that. Because my older sister and I were the oldest children, we took on a lot of responsibilities for Cathy.

We took care of her a lot; we babysat with her a lot. I can remember so many days when I was just so impatient, so indifferent. I wanted to go outside and play. I did not want to have to sit around and take care of Cathy. I can remember even sometimes while I was changing her clothes, she would start crying or become frustrated and maybe I would spank her.

She is very jumpy, and sometimes for reasons that I am not sure of, I would go up and scare her. And she would start to cry and I would hold her in my arms until I could make her laugh again. I know it was just my own frustrations, being taken out on her because I was being confined.

Richard: That makes me think of something. My wife, who is the younger of two girls, tells me that when she was real small her sister used to go up to her, hit her and then hug her. Which is the same kind of thing, but they are both normal, and it makes me think that you would have done the same thing if everything were okay.

Diane: Perhaps.

Gary: I think this is the case like with your looking through the wall, something all children grow up with. Pulling a little prank on somebody two or three years old. Like, "See that mountain over there," and he says, "Yeah." "Well we are on that mountain right now. It is really twenty miles away." This is normal.

Richard: I am sure that it is normal.

Diane: But the pain is still there.

Gary: The pain on their part or on my part?

Richard: On my part for knowing that I did that.

Diane: Yes, if you could just have the chance to undo that, you would give anything.

Dr. K.: Gary is saying that "all kids do that" yet you still feel that you did a terrible thing.

Tracy: In some way they are at a disadvantage to you. It is like picking on somebody who is smaller.

Diane: They cannot fight back.

Richard: Not only smaller, but in some way impaired.

Gary: I do not know though, because this is like training them to put up with this sort of thing, which *they* especially are going to have to do. In a sense it is good, because if they do not have that when they do get out it is really going to hurt.

Diane: But that would not apply in my case. She was really very helpless, in fact still is.

Tracy: Even Mark, I do not know, I'm not certain that teasing around home would have helped him to cope with others better. He is just such an open person, such a loving person, a trusting person. He will literally do anything for anyone, and not with malicious intent, just because he thinks that he is being friendly.

Richard: I wonder how much of the guilt that I feel is from that, which then influences my behavior toward him now. I wonder if I would sometimes do things that otherwise I would not, but that it is just that guilt itself that is motivating me to do it.

Diane: Like what?

Richard: OK, one example is the other night. I had a lot of studying to get done and he came over. He had gone out, and the friends that he was going to meet did not show up or something. And he decided to come over to our house and sat there. We chatted. As a matter of fact, my wife gets along with him much better than I do. She is much more spontaneous towards him. She is much more willing to treat him as a twenty-one year old person than I am. The television is on and the hockey game started. And I do not watch hockey games, but he does. And he started to get involved in it. I could not get up and go in the other room and study. I could not say to him, "Well, gee! I have to study." It is a small place anyway. If I said it to him, he probably would have understood, just like anybody else.

Gary: You just do not want to risk him not understanding.

Richard: That is right. In that way, I guess to some extent my guilt is for the way I treated him in the past. But also it is just that I do not want him to think that I do not like him or something. And it makes me do things that I probably would not do in another case.

Dr. K.: Diane talked about having to do extra chores or babysit more than you think you would have otherwise. Were there things that you felt were "extra" things that you had to do, that you would not have had to do if you did not have a disabled brother or sister?

Tracy: Well, my brother was involved in this exercise program in Philadelphia. From very early on he had to do eye exercises and things like that. It was a game to help him. As I got older, sometimes I felt it was an imposition on my time, but it was not that big a deal timewise. Whereas with you, Diane, babysitting—that involves a lot more time. I was always happy to do it. It was fun. It was a game.

Diane: I resented it once in a while, I think. Well, there are five girls in my family so that we were fortunately able to take turns. Of course, there were arguments here and there. I think you will find that anywhere. But as

I said, once in a while I do not know if I resented Cathy, or if I resented my parents. I am not really sure. I know I felt that the activities of our entire family, in terms of recreation, were restricted.

I was sort of active in grammar and junior high school doing a few things—playing basketball and being involved generally. It always hurt me when my parents were never able to come to watch me participate. I felt that they did not care about what I was doing, what my so-called accomplishments were. Of course the excuse always was, "Well, you know we cannot find a babysitter, and you will just have to accept that."

But I did not accept it at the time, and I really thought, "Well, they do not care. They just do not want to go, they could find a baby sitter if they really wanted to, but . . . ."

Dr. K.: Did you have similar experiences?

Gary: Not more so than normal, because, as I said before, we both have a five year old brother. So if you babysit for one brother who is five . . . . When you are babysitting for one, you babysit for both.

Tracy: I think the point that Diane brought up though, is that you were feeling somehow resentful because they were more special than you. And you feel, "God that is sick!" because look at him and look at me and how much more fortunate I am. On the other hand it does seem, sometimes, your parents are really paying a lot more attention, and deservedly so, to the other person.

Dr. K.: At the time you do not have this understanding view.

Diane: No.

Tracy: You know that you should not be feeling that way, but you do anyway. You knew, didn't you, you understood?

Diane: Well, yes, half of me understood and half of me did not. I wanted them there, and it seemed at the time that that was the most important thing. I always felt that certainly someone, some neighbor, someone who knew the family quite well, could watch Cathy for two or three hours.

But in retrospect, I realize that her physical condition was such that it was almost more than my parents could handle; certainly it was one which a neighbor would not feel very comfortable handling. Cathy used to have falling spells—they are not really convulsions—she would lose her balance. It was really quite scary for other people to see. I realize now that *that* was the biggest problem, it really was her physical condition which made getting her a babysitter difficult. It was *not* that they did not want to be there, but I did not realize that at the time.

Richard: One thing that still remains in my own mind is that when I was about nineteen or twenty, I ran away from home—a big deal kind of thing—it was very important to me. I stayed with some people down at the beach. For some reason, my father came looking for me. One of the other people who was living in that house saw him and got to talking to him, but did not tell him where I was. He came back and told me how my father was very upset and how I did not have to come back, but just to call and let him know that I was okay.

So, I called, and I talked on the phone with my father for about two hours, telling him every thing that bothered me, about my independence and all this other stuff. And he said, "Yeah, yeah that's right, I should have told you about sex, but I didn't." He said all that stuff and at the very end of the conversation he said one thing to me—I do not remember all of the other stuff in detail, but this one thing I remember. He said he had the feeling that "whenever I was giving some sort of affection or attention to your brother, you would get jealous." It hit me like a ton of bricks, because that had never never come into my mind at all. What do you *mean*, jealous? And I guess that I am still thinking about it now. A couple of weeks ago we went to my parents' house for supper. My father was talking to my brother, and I was watching. All of a sudden I pulled back and asked myself, "Are you jealous?" The whole thing came up to me right then, and I do not know; I am paying attention to it. I just sometimes wonder if my behavior shows that I was jealous of that and I cannot recognize it on any level.

Diane: I was wondering whether or not you felt the disabled child made your family especially close, or if you felt a sort of *specialness* about your family?

Dr. K.: Is that something you experienced?

Diane: Yes, I did very much so. I always felt that there was something very different about our family. Of course, you know, Cathy being that difference. Because of her difference there was a degree of specialness or closeness about us that, I do not know, it was sort of a bond that made us all very, very close. We all pitched in and helped each other out and Cathy was the one thing in difficult times that we could focus on. I was just wondering if any of you had that . . . .

Gary: I do not know. It is rather difficult to say. Our family has not been very close. Through Paul, yes, I would say that the family has gotten a little bit closer than it would have otherwise. He is the one who probably reaps the most attention. Outside of that, I do not think so.

Richard: I think you are fortunate. I think that our family was somewhat torn apart for that very reason. I guess it is something that I have no right to understand.

My mother feels that it was her fault that my brother was born the way he was. Some kind of drug I think that was being given out at that time, the early 50's, I think Thalidomide, that she seems to . . . maybe she took it, or that has something to do with it, she really feels it is something in herself. Sometimes I feel that my father has not addressed himself to that. It enhances his role as father, as a protective figure. He has a watchful eye out all the time, for my brother's financial affairs, social affairs, and everything else. He really has not attended that much to my mother's feelings, which bothers me.

I remember one time we had an argument about religion because I did not want to go to church anymore. They kept telling me that I had to go, and I said, "Well one thing is, why should I go when you don't go?" The conversation started to get a little bit intense. My mother kind of mumbled, but she clearly said, "Why? After what God did to me?" She ran into the other room, and started crying. At the time, I could not handle her, I felt like going in there and kind of consoling her, and saying—I do not know what I would have said—"It's okay."

Tracy: Are you the only other child?

Richard: No, there are two younger. There are three including Jim.

Tracy: I know that all you others have other siblings. Sometimes I felt, especially with my brother being the oldest and being the boy child, that my father wanted a boy child, and he expected me to go out and play baseball with him and do all the things that a boy child would do. Also, he was very concerned with developing my intellect. He is a really intelligent person and he wanted that in a child, to have some kind of identification that way.

Dr. K.: Was that something that you were aware of at that time?

Tracy: Well, I became more and more aware of it, I think it started to be apparent when Mark was not included in certain things. When I was younger, Mark would always go out and play ball with us, but now that we get into more things, most of our interaction is verbal. I find Mark being left out a lot. I think that it is just a carry-over. My father just wants me to be what Mark should have been. Maybe you all do not have that kind of experience. You are not the only other child.

Gary: Mother is going to shoot me for this, but she treats Paul and the way he is—she lets him get away with things. I do not think that it is right. I think that you should treat him as though he were like any other little boy.

When he does something wrong, she might not do this, but *I* will: I will scold him for it. Then, on the other hand, when he does something right, I will go out of my way to praise him for it.

Dr. K.: Is that something you noticed—that your parents disciplined you differently from your brother or sister?

Gary: Yes.

Diane: Not so much in my case. In fact, of course, mother had five children, and we were all quite young, she had us one right after another. She would sometimes spank Cathy, not hard of course, or slap her on the hand when she got into mischief, because she crawled and she is into absolutely everything that you can imagine. She is like an infant who wants to explore different things and see what is going on. When I saw Mother doing that, I did not like it, I wanted to protect Cathy. I was the one who felt, well, she does not understand, she should not be punished. One the other hand, there were times when I did the same thing. I lost my patience and I would punish Cathy, by either scaring her and making her cry or slapping her hand or spanking her for something. I always resented it, however, when I saw either one of my other sisters doing the same thing, or when I saw my mother disciplining her. I did not like that at all.

Richard: Like you had a special understanding of it.

Diane: Yes, it was almost like that. I did not think that it was fair, yet I knew that I did it myself sometimes.

Dr. K.: One of the things that people like yourselves talk about is whether or not their parents talk to them about their brother or sister. What were your experiences?

Tracy: You mean to explain the disability?

Dr. K.: Yes, could you talk . . .

Gary: You mean take us aside . . .

Dr. K.: Yes, what was done?

Gary: I think the fact that he was there was explanation enough. We could see. This is the way it was.

Richard: Nobody ever said anything special.

Diane: We never had family conferences, really, about her disability. I know that mother used to say to us if anything ever happened to me or your father, make sure that Cathy is well taken care of. Other than that, not much was said. We all knew that she would never really get any better, so it was just a matter of care.

Richard: I have said to myself—neither of my parents have ever mentioned it to me—as a matter of fact quite recently too, that I would be quite willing to take my brother and have him live with myself and my wife. I would not take, I would really have to be pressured before I would take either my wife's mother or my own parents to live with us for the rest of their lives. But my brother—I feel a lot differently about that.

Tracy: I think that is something that we all probably have thought about. I had never really thought about it until my father did take me aside one day, and said, "Listen, I want you to look at my will." I said, "Do I have to?" He said, "I think that it is time that you realized that you are the executrix of the will, even though you are the younger daughter, and you are in charge of your brother, and his protection." I thought of it before, but it had never really been all laid down on paper before me that I was responsible, which I do not mind.

Dr. K.: Do you think that there could have been some discussion earlier or that you wished you would have had a chance to talk about this when you were younger?

Richard: I felt no special urge.

Gary: I think not.

Diane: Well, we talked about it. It was not that the subject was ever avoided. It never seemed to take on any special importance because the other children were discussed too. It was just one of those family discussions that families have. It was not really different from anything else.

Dr. K.: We started with this earlier—what did you say when other kids would ask you, "What is the matter with your brother or sister?" How did you know what to say?

Richard: Somewhere along the line someone must have said to me that your brother was born that way, so when other people would ask me, I would say, "He was born that way," and it was kind of left at that. Sometimes I have marvelled over the boldness, I have never done it to anybody else, but it feels to me like boldness when someone comes up and says, "Hey, what happened to your brother?" Maybe because it seems so obvious to me. If you test the hypothesis that he got his arm cut off, you can very clearly see that this is not the case, and there is only one other alternative that I know of, so why the hell did you have to ask?

Diane: A lot of my friends asked, in fact all of them sooner or later. Of course, Cathy's condition was very obvious on sight. I always explained that Cathy was retarded and that she was born that way. Usually it was not pursued much beyond that, but, I never really resented the questions. I almost felt when I was younger that her condition required some sort of explanation.

I would bring friends into my home, and I would introduce, particularly when I was dating, my family, then I would introduce Cathy and say, "This is my retarded sister." I can remember young men coming in and walking over and saying "Hello, Cathy," and of course she could not talk. I had embarrassing moments. In fact there were times when I even wished that she would be in bed when my dates came over, because I did not want to explain. I was not so sure that I would be seeing these people again. I do not know, it was not that I felt that it was not any of their business. I thought that if this person is not going to be a friend, a close friend, why should they know, why should they be bothered with it?

Dr. K.: Did you feel that Cathy interfered with your social life?

Diane: No, not really. As I said, all of my friends, my close friends, took time with Cathy. They played with her, they held her because she was like an infant, they sang songs to her. In fact, many times when I was babysitting and I had my friends over, we would all sit around and play records—Cathy loves music—and we would all jump around and have a pretty good time with her.

Dr. K.: What about your teenage social life?

Tracy: Well, Mark was normal enough that he admired my dating life, and the first thing he would say to people—anybody, was "Boy, Tracy is going out with all these guys," you know, and that is great. He thought that was fantastic. But in a way, I grew up before he did. He dates now, but, you know, I think that he always looked up to me like an older sister type figure and I do not think that he resented my dating. He loved to be around the guys I was with, because they took an interest in him.

Dr. K.: Did you feel something interfering?

Tracy: No, I never did because he looked normal enough so unless they got into a discussion people would not realize anything was wrong with him. With people that I know are going to be around him for a long time, I will say, "You have to draw him out," or, "He is interested in sports, why don't you bring him out that way?" I never felt any need with acquaintances because he is normal enough.

Richard: Now that I think of it, my friends were pretty much supportive to me by being very friendly with him. Except one time, now I remember, one time, there was a kid who hung around with us who was very muscular and very conscious of it all the time, always displaying his abilities. One night, down at the park, he said, my brother had just walked by and he came up to me and said, "There is your brother!" like this [imitating his short arm]. I do not know now what I did, but the next thing, I knew I found myself up against a tree and he was again performing one of his physical feats. He had me around the tree, he had his foot on the tree and I was on the other side and he was pulling my arms. And there was nothing that I could do about it, not a goddamn thing, and I do not know, maybe if I had gotten another shot at him . . .

Tracy: The thing is, nobody is going to be your friend who makes fun of your sibling.

[Agreement by all]

If they react poorly, you know that they are not worth it.

Dr. K.: You certainly had some hard times, hard moments that were very moving.

Gary: I do not know, I cannot agree with what we came up with before, somebody who reacts poorly to it and you just shut them off. That is part of the problem right there, because they do not understand in the first place what it really is. If you shut them off, you are adding to it, you are dealing with fire with fire, and that is not the way to do it. Explain to them, if they do not understand that they in their own way . . .

Richard: Well, what should I have said to that person when he did that?

Gary: Well, as you put it, the next thing that you knew you were around the tree . . .

Tracy: But he knew about his brother, what more is there to explain then that he has a problem and you do not make fun of people that . . .

Gary: It does take a lot of patience, but this is part of it too.

Tracy: I agree, but you should be able to handle it, without these strong emotions, but . . .

Dr. K.: I wonder if that is really possible. The fury that you feel is a human feeling, to be so angry that someone is hitting you where it hurts and yet Gary is saying at the same time that if you put them off, then you never really will deal with it.

Richard: Yes, I agree with you, but what is there of substance or of some significance other than to say, well, he is different and he is handicapped in these obvious ways and you should not make fun of it? What is there of significance that you can say?

Gary: It is rather whimsical in this country—everybody says: Be independent! Be different! But when you get somebody who really is, everyone stares at him.

Dr. K.: Be different, but do not be *too* different.

Gary: Yeah, along certain guidelines it is okay.

Diane: You know, when you see someone you know quite well, and to feel that they are ridiculing or making fun of your sister or brother: Wow!

Certainly none of my friends ever teased or ridiculed Cathy, but I had acquaintances who would make fun of her, imitate her. She could not talk, she made noises. When they made fun of her it would be just a complete turn-off. I felt that if they had lived this long and could not deal with things any better than that . . . I mean you can *almost* understand if they are a person who has never been exposed to people who have had special problems.

Gary: This is the case with so many people.

Diane: Yes, it is true, this is the case but to do it in front of *me*, to imitate her noises, to imitate her spastic motions, how can you make a person like that understand? *What* do you say?

Dr. K.: Did you have the experience of knowing other families with disabled children?

Tracy: I did through this patterning thing. You have like a teamwork system. Each person is responsible for an arm or a leg. You need people, so you kind of band together and help each other out. That is how I had contact with other people, but not on the street where I live. I did not know any other people with disabilities.

Dr. K.: Was that when you were older?

Tracy: Yes, in my young teens.

Diane: I did not, when I was in grade school, or even high school. I have since met different people in families who have disabled siblings, but not at the time I was growing up with Cathy.

Dr. K.: Two of you are married. What special issues came up when you were thinking of getting married: your spouses' reactions and so forth?

Richard: Like I said before, I am much more inhibited with my brother than my wife is.

Dr. K.: Was that true before you married as well?

Richard: Yes. Oh! I see what you mean. There was not that much contact between my family and my wife before we were married, so there was not really that much opportunity for it.

Now I am afraid sometimes to say things, to make casual jokes about drinking and getting drunk, drugs, sex, the whole bit, because I am afraid that it might put my brother on the wrong path, but my wife sees the whole thing a lot differently. She is more willing to treat him normally, normal to an extent that—I just . . . I do not know—because of my position or what, I just cannot do it.

Dr. K.: How was it telling the person that you had decided to marry about your brother?

Richard: I remember one thing when my brother went away to school. It was a long drive. Sometimes he would come home on weekends and my wife and I would take him back. I guess, come to think of it, she did not spend all that much time, when we got there, with Jim.

I would go with my brother from the car into his room and chat with him for a few minutes, make sure that everything was okay. She would wait in the car. The very first time I was with her, I came out, I got into the car, and I drove about a quarter of a mile or so. I stopped the car and I just started crying, and I just could not stop, I just could not. The whole thing: it was just too much.

She said to me something like, "You know that this is a very good thing that is happening for him; he is fortunate to have such a good experience." We drove another quarter of a mile and *she* started crying. It is very . . . sometimes it is pretty hard to say—to see this as good. *Sure* this is good, but what is ahead?

Another thing: when my brother comes over, if my wife has like a housecoat on, or whatever, sometimes I see him catch little peeks here and there. It shows me that he has a sex drive and that another aspect of a person's being human is a sex drive. I guess I have had to marvel over it to some extent, to realize further just how normal he is. He really is just like all the rest of us.

Gary: This is the way I feel they *should* be treated. If you treat them as normal, they will respond as such. If you treat them as abnormal, they will respond as such. Of course there is a degree you have to deal with, you know there are always the extremes.

Dr. K.: What was it like for you with your husband?

Diane: Well, when I met my husband my sister had already been institutionalized. He had never been exposed, really, to families who had retarded or disabled people, and of course I told him about it. We became very close very quickly and he came to know my family quite well. He took a ride with us one Sunday afternoon up to see her and they got along famously.

His reaction was very very good. He held her and he played with her and things were fine, but we started talking, in fact are still talking to this day, about . . . I know I have a fear of pregnancy because of Cathy.

Because he has never been exposed to people who are retarded and who are disabled in some way, he seems to feel, especially about people like Cathy that they would be better off not having been born because they are so severely retarded. You know, if you can do something about it, if you *know* they are going to be born this way, why let them be born? He feels that their life is being lived for no reason at all. It is difficult for him to understand it because he has never been around her. He cannot see that her joy in life is playing with people, listening to music or being well. Her joys are simply not what our joys are.

I have often wondered, in fact I have often talked to him about what would happen if I had a retarded child.

He could not understand in the first place why she was at home for seventeen years, not realizing some of the burdens and some of the problems that go along with that, not really understanding, not really appreciating the joys, too, that come along with having a child like that.

The thought of immediately institutionalizing a child—I do not think I could do that because of my experiences with Cathy. We have had some rather heated arguments about it. I do not know what would happen. He does not understand it because he has not been around it, he did not live with her for the years I lived with her, and he cannot see the reason for her existence.

Of course, I naturally feel differently having been so close to her for so long. He gets along with her beautifully, but he seems to think that the world would be better off, that those people would be better off, people in Cathy's condition anyway, if they simply did not exist. I am sure there are many people who feel this way, but I do not know, I certainly do not think that I could institutionalize a youngster if I had . . .

Tracy: I agree. If it were something where you knew the child was going to be born handicapped, you could abort; that is a different issue.

Diane: Yes, that's one thing.

Tracy: But once you have the child—then having to see things, like stories about Willowbrook and places like that, where my doctor suggested my brother to be sent. To think that he could be in a cart, where now he has got a college education, is really phenomenal!

Diane: I know we did not realize that Cathy was retarded until she was six months old. In that six months, of course, there was a tremendous attachment. I do not know, it is difficult to deal with. I do not know what I would do about it, really.

Gary: I think it comes down to two problems. Of course, you have medical problems of the child. The science of medicine is going to deal with them eventually. The other problem, is having other people exposed to it. Once you are exposed to it you really know what it is. Then you are not that worried about it.

I think that this is a step forward, we are making an effort here to "spread the word," or whatever. They are like anybody else no matter how bad off they are. They want love; they want affection. We send them off to an institution, or whatever, they are not going to get this. The most important thing is the happiness of the child. If we can get other people to understand this, half the battle will be won.

Diane: Well, I do not really agree with you when you say they do not get love and care in institutions. We all know of many institutions that probably should just be blown up and started all over again, but there are others that are quite good. I know we are very fortunate with the institution that Cathy is in. Of course, she requires custodial care and she gets that, she gets very good care, but because she has such a sweet disposition—she laughs all the time, she's a *delightful* person—the nurses absolutely love her. They are always having birthday parties and all the other patients are there. You know, she is really sort of the center of attention. Although the family does not really know whether or not she recognizes us when we come to see her—there is really no way of knowing that I guess—she seems to be just as happy with the love and attention and care the nurses give her, which is really a great deal.

It seems that they would rather take up time with Cathy than with some of the other patients who are older. These are people who are on up into their sixties who do not seem to laugh and do not really seem to enjoy much of anything.

Gary: What do you think? Let me put it on a different footing. They do not usually get as much love and attention in an institution as they would get at home.

Diane: That is true.

Dr. K.: What do you think it has been like for your parents through their lives?

Gary: Before and after?

Dr. K.: Yes.

Gary: I think it's sort of agonizing for them, in a way, because the job of the parent is to bring the child up, and train him so that he will be able to go out on his own, to spread his wings and fly. Of course, when you have a special problem like this, it is much, much more difficult. To get down to the emotional level, I do not know, I have never experienced it.

Richard: I can remember a few different things that are kind of strung together that make up some sort of statement. First, that my brother was sitting at the table one day: he was goofing off, really playing around and stuff. My father had come home a bit short-tempered and he just, what he meant to do, and I really believe that he just meant to do it, was to just tap my brother in the back of the head to make him stop. But the tap in the back of the head caused his head to go down and hit the table. He chipped a tooth. It is very hard to explain the reaction that my father had; it was just incredible. He went into the other room and cried, which is something that my father does not do very often. I think he has reached a kind of balance now, where as far as his protective role is concerned it is not a reaction thing anymore, like, "get away and just let him fall down," you know, or "just make life easy for him." That is not the case anymore. It is more like he wants my brother to feel the burdens and the joys of life like all the rest of us.

My mother: it is very funny the way my mother reacts to the whole thing. On the one hand, she wants him to grow and do all the things that any one does. On the other hand, my father has to hold her in the background and then let Jim out of the house, you know? I mean, if he wants to move out and she does *not* want him to, that's all there is to it! And my father *does* want him to. I think she is still in the thing where she wants just to protect him.

Tracy: My mother is like that too because our father has been working. She has really had the burden of taking him to the hospitals, and being with him when he is having his seizures, and fighting with the school principals to keep him *in* school, and fighting with doctors to keep him *out* of institutions. My father has been somewhat shielded from all that, except the agony of having to decide what exactly we are going to do, and how we are going to help this kid have a life of his own. . . . Just the financial burden is tremendous! Your parents are probably no strangers, too, going to doctors and special schools and institutions.

Richard: Yes, I can remember many times seeing my mother sit by the phone with numbers all over the place and phone books from all over the country just to get a little help, going through all this stuff. This guy was supposed to call back, he had some new thing. One time I think somebody really *did* something that in the end really hurt my parents. This doctor said that he could remove some tissue, some nerve, from another part of his body and put it in his ears, in the auditory canal, whatever it is. Just despite themselves, they got all excited, and then they came to find out this guy was a quack. That really did hurt.

I remember something else. Near one of the police stations in town there is a store where they sell artificial arms and legs. Very much against my brother's will, when he was about seven or eight, they took him there and tried to . . . I remember! We sat there for the whole day and fitted arms on him. You know, "Do like this!" "No, a hook is no good because that doesn't look good in public." "Would you like an electronically controlled . . . . " They *did* buy one. My brother never wore it and I do not even know where it is. I think it is just disgusting.

Diane: I had a similar experience, or my parents did, with doctors. About a year ago they went up to visit Cathy. I guess they met with some sort of specialist who told Mother and Daddy that they thought Cathy could be taught to walk with a couple of operations: a little of this and a little of that. Needless to say, the entire family was sort of shocked and stunned by the whole thing. We were very excited about it, but then again we thought, "Well, all these years have passed—why did we not do something or should we have done something ten years ago, twenty years ago?" We got a call about one or two weeks later saying that no, they were sorry that, indeed, it was not possible. We just hated the man so much for doing something like that—why?

Richard: I know, they put my brother in the hospital once. The nerves in the four fingers that he has are short, they are too short, so he cannot stretch his fingers out all the way. Some brilliant fool got the idea that he could, well, he figured it was not the nerves; it was the skin, the skin was too tight!

So they brought him to the hospital and they made a skin graft for his fingers and then for two or three weeks after that they waited—well, after it healed enough they devised some sort of mechanism that would be put on the back of his hand to help keep it straight.

My mother tried. It was an "If there's a chance, I'll do it" kind of thing. But that kid walked around the house for two weeks just crying, crying, crying because it hurt; it *really* hurt. Maybe somehow he knew that this is foolishness, it is not going to work. I can remember myself saying, "What are you doing that for? That's the way he is, just accept that instead of trying to make him into something else."

Dr. K.: I wonder if, somewhat at the risk of diverting you—the thing you are talking about is so moving, yet, at the same time—I kind of wonder what would you tell young kids, who are in the situation you were in, if you were in a sense giving advice to families, children and parents. What are some of the things you would try to say to them?

Diane: That's a very difficult question. It's *extremely* difficult. I know in my own particular case Cathy was easily accepted, just treated as a regular family member. She was just sort of the child who would always be an infant. We realized that there were certain things that had to be done and certain responsibilities that as a family we all had to share in and help each other with. We tried to do it as best we could, I guess, and with as little. . . . I do not know if I am really in a position to give advice. I am not so sure that things worked out very well in terms of my own feelings, in terms of where I am at in my own head about it. I have fears, I have doubts, I have guilt feelings about certain things I did. I wish many times I could go back and do it over again. So I do not know if I could really give advice to anyone else.

Dr. K.: Well, what would you do over?

Diane: Just little tiny things—the punishing . . .

Richard: That is right, they are such little things that are important.

Diane: That are not so tiny, that are not so tiny at all.

Dr. K.: What specifically are you talking about?

Richard: I would not have said to my brother I can see through the wall and you cannot. In a way, that is like stating, in a symbolic way, the reality of the situation, isn't it? I have a physical ability that you do not. Do you understand? Do you know what I mean?

Dr. K.: I understand what you are saying, but I am wondering, would you advise a five year old not to tease his sibling? You really could not. I understand what you are saying, but . . .

Diane: I would advise it. I mean I would advise young children to—I would advise it, I do not know if they are going to follow the advice—to try and have a great deal of patience, because you are not aware of it at the time, but it makes such a difference when you get older. I know when I see Cathy now, it is always terribly upsetting for me. I usually come home in tears. I look at her and I say, "Oh, if I had only had that day again, if I could do it over again."

Richard: Something you said at the very beginning impressed me. I realize we are on another topic, and I just want to mention it so we do go back. You said that as time goes on now it is getting more difficult for you to see her. Do you think it is because you are realizing—you see things in a broader context?

Diane: I think part of the reason is that she is in an institution and I do not see her very much. I think if I were with her everyday, of course I am not at home anymore, if she *were* at home, if I were able to go back home and see her there and to *know* that she is getting care, to be able to make her laugh again. I think it would make a difference. I think one of the issues is that I am separated from her. I do not really know what is happening to her every day. I cannot call my mother and say well, gee, how is Cathy doing today. Maybe it is because I am getting older. I do not know.

Richard: I feel that towards *all* my younger brothers.

Diane: Yes, that is true.

Richard: Whenever I go home for supper or something I notice. Like my little brother showing me his train set, it is all constructed now, it is all done. I mean if I lived there I would have seen the box of tracks . . .

Diane: I think it is being away. I feel it with my younger sisters. I feel a hurt there, some sort of pain that I am not around when they could really use me. They are growing up and they could use a big sister to look up to right now. Although they do when I am there, it is certainly not like being home every day.

Richard: Now that you are out of the house and you are on your own what *is* your relationship to your younger brothers and sisters? I feel that when one of my brothers kept asking me, "Can we go out and play catch, can we go out and play catch?" And meanwhile I am trying to communicate with my father, which is something we had a lot of trouble doing before we got married, and trying to pay attention to all this other stuff, so in the end I feel—I went home and felt that I did not pay any attention to my little brother, my youngest brother.

Diane: It is so encouraging to hear that, I thought I was the only one. I go through that . . .

Richard: My wife suggested two things. First, you are not peanut butter, you cannot be spread all over the place. But the other thing is that we have our own life to live. If we think that we are going not only to live our own lives, but make life easier for somebody else, to some extent we are keeping them from the possibility of going through life on their own.

Dr. K.: The "peanut butter" thing, and what you said at the end sort of characterizes the struggle of your parents as well as your own struggle. If only I could do a little more, and yet, at the same time, I have to hold back and give them an opportunity to grow. Just as your parents probably went through with you . . .

Tracy: It is just so much easier with someone who is normal. I mean you always feel that you have to protect them somehow. I think my parents feel that even now. Mark has a job and he commutes and he does all these things, but he is still living at home. There is still that huge break that he has to make and it seems almost harder for my parents to make than for Mark.

Richard: It is much much more difficult for my parents. After Jim left that school out of state, he wanted to live there. As a matter of fact he still wants to. Sometimes on weekends, he goes there. He knows people there and he likes them and the area. Many times he says that he wants to live there. My parents think, especially my mother, that it is really great. If he said I want to look for an apartment I think they would say there are no apartments. But meanwhile what you are actually doing is denying the possibility.

Tracy: That is another problem though just in American society, well, in any society. There really is no provision made for handicapped people to live lives of their own. I think that that is something that *has* to be done.

Gary: What do you mean by living life on their own?

Tracy: For example, it would be very helpful for my brother to get an apartment by himself, but there are certain things he would have trouble doing, like balancing a checkbook maybe, or handling rent agreements. You just do not want him to be used by people. But if there were some kind of apartment complex or something that had people with similar problems that could group together and be helped by certain people that are professionals that can deal with this . . .

Gary: This is what I was wondering—putting them out on their own—in the society, off in a special group. I wonder . . .

Tracy: Well, to some extent they have to be helped by people, so they cannot be totally independent. But still I think they need to be separated from family. They cannot be infants all their lives, especially if they have some skills and can hold a job.

Gary: That is right. Finding that middle path between taking their blows for them, and leaving enough for experience.

Tracy: Yes. But there is no choice now. It is either home or institution. I think we need some other choices that would be between those two that would allow people to be independent, to have some autonomy.

Richard: That presupposes the kind of understanding that you are asking for.

Gary: It does. There is an awful lot of misunderstanding.

Dr. K.: Many parents talk about institutionalization because of their other children.

Richard: As a protective measure?

Tracy: So the other kids do not have to be penalized.

Dr. K.: You are saying, though, that *you* could do it, *you* could face it.

Diane: I think that speaking from my own life, it has been a tremendous experience insofar as my personal growth goes. It made our family extremely close. We have some sort of special bond between us that we share, and *will* share for the rest of our lives. I cannot imagine life without Cathy. I feel that it has been marvelous for Cathy as well as for everyone involved. We have learned so very much, we have developed patience and understanding.

Gary: You mentioned before that "because of other children." Do you mean within the family or without?

Dr. K.: Within.

Gary: I find that bad because, granted it may be an idea, but this would be a welcomed experience to teach the other children within the family to understand.

Richard: Yes, I am saying about the same thing. Why deny the rest of those normal people the chance to learn a lot about themselves while they are learning a lot about those other people as well?

Diane: It is just like with normal siblings. You are going to have children, normal siblings, who—you are going to have your ups and downs. Any children with any parents: you are going to have your bad days and your good days. You are going to have problems with one child in one area and maybe different problems with another child in another area. Life is not perfect. People are not perfect, and you just have to accept that and live with it and learn to deal with it. There is an awful lot to learn from it, I think.

Tracy: I think you learn very quickly that there is someone else besides "me." That is a hard lesson for a child to learn.

Dr. K.: You may face it again with your own children.

Richard: That is the thing that happens to me. Some of the feelings that you mentioned before. Well, no maybe I cannot say that.

Dr. K.: What?

Richard: The possibility that . . .

Diane: That you could have a—the same child?

Richard: Yes. That is it. You know there could be something defective in me as well.

Tracy: In a family you follow your instincts. I am not so much concerned with other kids who might have the problem later. I am concerned with the other people around who do not have the problem and do not know how to deal with it, because they do not have the basic instinct of love, protection and family unit to worry about.

Richard: But I think the point is, or the reason I bring it up is, to make notice of the extreme complexity that there is. It is probably even further complicated by the love that you have.

Dr. K.: I feel very drained. How much more is there to say?

Forgotten Children

Meyer Schreiber

This article is adapted from the keynote speech delivered by Professor Schreiber at "The Forgotten Children—A Conference Designed to Explore the Everyday Relationships of Children in a Family with their Handicapped Brothers and Sisters as They Grow and Develop." The conference, held on April 5, 1974, at Rhode Island College, was sponsored by The National Foundation-March of Dimes, The Easter Seal Society (Meeting Street School) and Rhode Island College.

The italicized statements in the article were excerpted from a panel discussion at the same conference moderated by Dr. Stanley D. Klein, Editor-in-Chief of *Exceptional Parent* magazine. The panel included four siblings of persons with disabilities and a parent.

Today in America there is much speculative talk and soul searching about the family. What is the function of family life? What is its future? Not only do our daily press, television and radio reflect this concern, but professional journals and popular magazines likewise have directed considerable attention to such questions as they describe, discuss and dissect family life today.

New variations such as single-parent families or communal households have made us more aware, and even self-conscious, of the family as one of the basic institutions of our society. The increase of women in the work force, changing sex role definitions and patterns of child care, rising divorce rates and declining birth rates—all of these, in one way or another, reflect new values, new moralities and new ways of living. They suggest that the family is in a state of transition, or at any rate that a fundamental re-evaluation is called for. Who among us has not been moved by these developments to consciously consider or reconsider our hopes, our desires, our expectations or the quality of our lives not only for ourselves but for our children as well?

WALL OF SILENCE

Yet with all this general outpouring there is a large gap, almost a wall of silence, when it comes to a meaningful discussion of the life of a family with a child who is disabled. The simple fact is that *our concept of the family does not include a place for the family with a child with a disability.* According to the traditional stereotypes, which have prejudiced all too many of us for far too long, such a family was out of the question—literally. Identified and "ruled out" by the presence of the disabled child. And what about the "normal" brothers and sisters of the disabled child? Where do they fit in the family? In the community?

It has taken many years, fraught with disillusion, frustration and the pain of outright rejection for parents and families to change the misconceptions and correct the myths which have dominated the beliefs and attitudes of many in this country about disabilities. Only now is the disabled child coming to be perceived as a human being with the same basic needs for love, acceptance and belonging as other children.

> My brother said this discussion (about siblings) was important because "I want people to know that I am a human being, that I am an individual and that I am good."

This gradual change has made it possible for parents, brothers and sisters, and others in the family to come forward and talk about their situations openly and honestly—with each other and with others. Families can confront what it means to have a child who is markedly different in their midst. Moreover, they are in a better position to get the special assistance and care that the special needs of their child require.

Most of the burden for creating this climate of change has been carried by the families concerned, with some assists from a small (but growing) network of friends and professionals. It goes without saying that this is not as it should be, that families with disabled children have more than their share to cope with, and that society at large has a responsibility to change and widen its circle of care and concern rather than place the burden for change on those affected.

STEREOTYPES DIE HARD

Our newspapers abound with all kinds of advice columns, ranging from how to grow a garden in the shade to how to deal with life stresses. Not too long ago, in my local newspaper, Ann Landers was asked about the proper response of a family friend to the birth of a retarded child.

"Should I send a card of congratulations in view of the child's condition?" the anxious friend wondered. Miss Landers' sensitive response was to do so by all means. "Your friend gave birth to a child who should be welcomed just like any other child."

In another column, several years ago, she was asked what to do about a next door neighbor's child, nine years old and retarded, who played with her child, seven years old and normal. The correspondent indicated that her husband was concerned about the "bad habits" their daughter could pick up from this association. Miss Landers' tender and thoughtful reply was that their daughter was learning more about human relations than many older people ever would, that her friendship with the neighbor child was teaching her the all-important lesson of living generously with others and accepting them and all of their differences.

But stereotypes and prejudices—as well as the fears that lurk behind them—die hard. These typical examples indicate the nature of the work to be done regarding educating and enlightening the average person about disabilities and how families live with them.

What we ourselves have learned—together and alone, as parents and professionals—is quite different from what we have been taught or led to expect. Of all the myths perpetuated by well-intentioned but misinformed, or inexperienced, or uninterested "others," none has been so prevalent as the myth that says a seriously disabled child can not live at home. "Institutionalize" was the emotionally charged key word in days past, and to some extent still today. Institutionalize was the standard advice: avoid the twin dilemmas of giving too much attention to the disabled child—and therefore too little to the other children—and becoming too attached to this child (as if this were a crime).

My folks were told that it might be wiser to put her in an institution and close the door so they could take care of the rest of us.

Gradually, with time and experience, we have learned differently. And we have, in fact, found that there are meaningful solutions, realistic alternatives and a wide range of possibilities for helping, for hope.

PROFESSIONALS' COMMITMENT

What is the task of professionals with respect to exceptional families? How do we translate our sense of commitment to social service, our belief in the dignity and worth of every individual, into effective work with these families who look to us for assistance with the particularly knotty problems they may face?

Very simply put, we give back to parents, to families, to "normal" sisters and brothers, to the disabled child, what we have learned from them. We have learned from: our contacts, casual or intensive; our observations, informal or formal; what the family tells us, individually or collectively, with or without words; and our talk and experience with them. We try to give back to the family: an increased awareness of each other as individuals, and as a family; a heightened sensitivity to their mutual concerns and problems and to the interdependence of their day-to-day existence; and a fuller understanding of the possibilities as well as the necessary limitations of their lives. We try to offer love, compassion and a commitment to action which we embody in what we do and what we feel.

When it comes right down to it, all that I have really learned, after satisfying the formal criteria of my training as a social worker, has come from my associations with individuals and families who have been my clients.

THE REST OF THE FAMILY

The child with a disability is a member of a family and of a community. Experience and research both suggest clearly that the problems of a disabled child are best dealt with in these "real life" contexts of family and community. But what about the rest of the family? How can parents best meet the needs of their other children as they too struggle through the everyday crises of growing up?

"Normal" siblings absorb and reflect parental attitudes and concerns: parents who deal with the presence of a disabled child in a positive fashion will generally find that the other children will too.

When John was born I was nine years old, and I guess some children might think that if they have a retarded child their life would sort of end, but I guess mine sort of began.

Parents' feelings, whether or not they are ever actually expressed in words, are unquestionably communicated. What is said and not said, what is done and not done—they miss very little. Children detect and reflect, often without being fully conscious of it, their parents' "true" feelings.

- I understood it from the beginning. My parents would go behind closed doors to talk about it. . . . My parents didn't really come right out and say it to me—I guess we don't communicate that well.
- I just couldn't see in my mind when I grew up why they weren't exactly telling me what it was.

Pretending or equivocating can cause more harm and confusion for the nondisabled children than it avoids. It is best to discuss in an open, honest way what you as parents feel and experience and what you expect of all your children. By all means, approach your children at their level of development and comprehension. Don't talk down to them, but don't pitch things over their heads either. In addition to keeping nondisabled children informed, this kind of straight talk is a means of genuinely sharing family concerns and actively involving children in family problems and decisions. It encourages them to take responsibility.

- You ask, when you are younger, about what his disability is and you are confused. You'll never really get a direct answer.
- My parents were very open and were very open with John himself. They explained it to him. He knows that he has a disability.
- . . . when my parents gave me responsibility, it made me feel that I was helping, I was contributing to the family.

Most children will benefit from straight talk, from a sense of sharing in vital family concerns with their parents whom they love and respect. Usually a simple, direct answer in response to a child's query helps more than a volume of involved and circuitous explanations.

Sometimes parents feel their nondisabled children need professional help simply because of the fact that they have a disabled brother or sister—or because they may react to special stresses in the family in unfamiliar or unacceptable ways. This, by itself, however, is not necessarily symptomatic. Such behavior may indeed be healthy and eventually constructive in that the child is not pushing his worries and questions down under, but letting them surface so that they can be faced and dealt with. Often a frank and sensitive discussion that acknowledges and credits the young person with being an intelligent, feeling brother or sister may do more than a load of professional advice and/or counseling.

Be clear about your expectations of your nondisabled children, and let them know what you expect. Do not expect a sibling to compensate or make up for what you may perceive to be the lacks in another child. Do not make of him or her an all too convenient baby sitter, automatic playmate, or inappropriate parent substitute. The support the other children can give, the responsibility they will feel, must come from inside (and from your example), not from an imposed caretaker role.

- Everybody kinda had the impression that I would take him wherever I went.
- In the beginning it was alright—I used to pull him down the street in the wagon . . . it wasn't that he had a disability or anything, it was just that he was my brother and he was a pain in the neck.

AWARENESS OF DEVELOPMENT

Parents must be aware of their nondisabled children's level of development as they attempt to involve these children in the special intimacies and efforts of the family. As the nondisabled child grows beyond infancy, he learns from those around him—his parents in particular—about the meanings of differences as they very personally relate to his disabled brother or sister. Here, parents need to provide help, direction, understanding and explanation. They need to inspire in their nondisabled offspring a sense of compassion and care without depriving or isolating these children from the experiences of everyday life or exposures to neighbors, classmates and others in the world outside the family.

- In cases where it was either I have to go or they have to go, they let me go out. They wouldn't deprive me of it. They would rather deprive themselves—in fact, they didn't even think that it is being deprived.
- I have my friends to make and he cannot hold me back.

There are specific issues which typically arise from stage to stage throughout the life cycle. The preschool and school-aged child, for example, will be concerned with attention—who gets how much—and may be particularly susceptible to hostile or jealous feelings toward the disabled sibling who requires and gets extra parental attention.

• I think in our family there was kind of the feeling that John might be allowed to get away with more or do more, where we would kind of be reprimanded or whatever.

• When I got to be around eight or nine years old and the doctor visits were still going on and it got more and more, I did start to feel very alone and I wondered, you know, why he was getting all this special attention.

The elementary school-aged child is apt to confront, and ask blunt questions about his sibling's "differences." He lives in a world of age-mates where even little differences between children assume enormous significance. Here, the primary family group needs to provide support, particularly for the youngster who seems unable to share his concerns and feelings openly.

• You'll see kids making fun of him within the neighborhood and I can feel myself tense right up. I want to go over and smash the kid. I think that's really something you have to deal with within yourself.

• Normal children do want to see if a handicapped person is real.

• My peers were very important to me right then and that was that—I just didn't want to have any little tag-alongs.

Teen-agers not only feel the "difference"—and may worry about it—they are relentlessly concerned about what their friends at school and in their social world will think. Adolescence can be a time of almost morbid self-consciousness. Here, parents are encouraged to "level" with their children about what their sibling's disability encompasses, how it affects them—and how it doesn't.

• And though you were younger, how do you explain this to people who come over to the house?

• At times we thought we were tied down in certain instances in our lives.

• When I got to be about dating age and boys came to the house, if there were inquiries about my mother, my father, my sister, I told them about my family. Donny is a member of the family and that was the perfect time for me to go on and tell them these things about his disability.

Parents have a responsibility to all their children to help them deal with those parts of the world around them that are unfriendly and harsh. Every community has many well intentioned people, but rejection wears many masks and hostility is often insensitively and inappropriately betrayed or expressed. The nondisabled child needs support from those closest to him in order to come to terms with this aspect of the "outside world."

The young adult is concerned about matters such as genetics (will it happen to me?) and expections of responsibility for the care of a disabled sibling should their parents die. Parents have to make their wishes clear in a realistic and reasonable way, taking into consideration each child's right to an independent adult family life.

   • If I were married or got married later on and my parents die, I will have to take him in.
   • If we have to, we'll take him in. But I would rather know that he could stand up alone—well not alone, but be able to go through life.
   • I thought that if it was going to make any difference to my fiancé, it was a very important thing to bring up.
   I told them about my family and that it was a package deal.

CHILDREN CAN TAKE CARE

Most of the brothers and sisters of disabled children I have worked with are very concerned about their exceptional sibling. They are loving, feeling and want to help. These young people have stressed their desire to learn "the facts of life" in the intimate, private family circle, from the people they know best and trust most. Moreover, they want to be involved in dealing with the day-to-day responsibilities and crises out of which families create their identity and vitality. They want to play an active role in family life—for all that means.

   • I got a different outlook on life and I really think that I'm lucky to have my brother.
   • I could still be the parent of a handicapped child and I have very positive feelings about this that it can work, that a family can stay together.
   • I think that since there is a handicapped child we have grown as people.

The presence in a family of a child with a disability poses certain particular problems for the nondisabled brothers and sisters, and for the parents as well, albeit in different ways. Yet all the dramatis personae on the family scene—parents, the disabled child, his sisters and brothers—are developing bonds of affection and loyalty for and with one another as they create and innovate new roles and relationships within the family and as they try to help others expand their own concepts of humanity and community.

PART II

Parents and Professionals

The nine articles that follow are by parents and professionals. Each conveys the practical wisdom that comes from being with children and trying to encourage and support each individual child. These articles do not address specific stages of child development, although most were written by mothers of children between the ages of five and ten. Each article offers useful information for parents, professionals, sisters, and brothers seeking suggestions to apply to their own lives.

By sharing experiences, observations, and approaches, the parent-written articles illustrate how parents develop unique expertise about their children and find creative ways to meet individual needs, while trying not to neglect their own needs as adults. Five of the parent articles describe family situations in which the child with a disability is the oldest child. Six of the parent articles were written when at least one child was already in elementary school. Each of the eight parents wrote in the midst of the everyday challenges of parenting two or three children including one child with a disability.

All parents want their children to love each other and to be kind and understanding of each other. All parents also know that the relationships between sisters and brothers, just like the relationships between husbands and wives, are not always loving, kind, or understanding. Fortunately, the interactions between sisters and brothers and the issues confronted by parents have a great deal in common from one family to the next, even when specific circumstances vary widely. These articles are valuable because they illustrate common sibling interactions when one sibling has a disability, and because the authors provide models of understanding and behavior for others to consider.

The arrival of the first baby changes the lives of new parents in many ways. When the first child is disabled, the lives of new parents are changed in more complicated ways. While all infants and young children require a great deal of parental attention and energy, the young child with a disability usually requires an even greater investment of attention, patience, energy, and time. As parents focus their attention on the child with special needs, a routine of early intervention programs, medical visits, and other special activities become "normal" for the family. Some parents devote tremendous energy into doing everything possible to assist the child's development. Within the family setting, the first child with a disability is perceived as "normal." Then, when a second child arrives on the scene without special needs, things change. As her younger son advanced developmentally, Paula M. Michalegko describes in "A Sibling Born *Without* Disabilities" how she was painfully reminded of the differences between her sons. Susanne Carter's experiences with her younger son and how he was developing enabled her to relax in her relationship with her older son who is mentally retarded. She no longer felt compelled to do so much and reports that her perspective became more realistic. In contrast, another mother, Victoria Leclerc Therrien, felt that her family's energies continued to be focused on her oldest son and, in that way, her younger son was penalized for being normal.

Each parent article discusses aspects of sibling relationships that are common in any family, but are likely to become exaggerated when one sibling is disabled:

- Fairness. Do parents give (attention, time, money, love) equally to each sibling?

- Expectations. Do parents have the same academic, social and/or behavioral expectations for each child?

- Rewards and punishments. How do parents respond to accomplishments or to inappropriate behavior?

- Caretaking responsibilities. Is one sibling responsible for the care or protection of the other, now or in the future?

- Negative feelings. How do parents respond to negative feelings between siblings?

In the eyes of many who have endured the human ups and downs of sibling relationships, the last four of the above are related to the first—being fair! Each article also addresses the issue that is unique to sibling relationships involving a sibling who is disabled or chronically ill: the need on the part of the sibling without a disability for information about the disability. Finally, each article provides examples that can assist readers in their efforts with their own children.

Because Victoria Leclerc Therrien, whose first child has Down syndrome, was concerned that her second son would be affected negatively by his older brother, she interviewed children about their feelings and their perspectives on how their lives had been enriched by having a sibling with a disability. Her interviews made clear the importance of complete information about a child's diagnosis, its causes, and its implications for the future. The process also made her an advocate of sibling groups.

Paula M. Michalegko's article emphasizes the impact of the sibling issues on parental feelings, especially how the advances of the "normal" sibling can remind parents of differences between their children. She describes how her desire to treat each child as an individual can be difficult. She also reminds parents that they, too, are human.

Via the title of her article, "When the Youngest Becomes the Oldest," Connie E. Post reminds us, as well as her daughter whose older brother has autism, that much of life is not fair. She also describes the dilemma for parents when a younger child imitates troubling behaviors of an older sibling.

In "Brothers With a Difference," the older sibling, Mark, is autistic. While Renee Seidenberg wants to encourage her sons' friendship, she also wants to protect her younger son from potential teasing and embarrassment because of Mark's behavior. She shares her questions about the future for both boys and identifies the need for children to voice their pain and frustrations.

As she watched and enjoyed her younger son develop normally, Susanne Carter and her husband no longer felt compelled to put so much energy into activities with their older son, Darwin, who is mentally retarded. Instead, she describes how this change enabled her to appreciate and enjoy Darwin for himself. In describing various activities with her sons, she notes how Darwin, in some ways, is easier to parent.

In "Christina Loves Katherine," the younger child is mentally retarded. Katherine Berg describes the strong bond between her daughters and identifies several factors that have contributed to their relationship. For example, she asks Christina and her friends to play with Katherine a while before they play by themselves and she encourages Christina to teach her younger sister. Not only has Berg continually explained Katherine's disability, she has taken Christina to Katherine's special class and made sure to point out the positive characteristics of each of Katherine's classmates.

"Is that Your Brother?" illustrates how Nancy Schmalz decided to prepare Brian, her older son, for the comments of other children about his brother, Daniel, who is physically disabled and mentally retarded, by teaching Brian's second grade class about Daniel. She also hoped to encourage Brian to take on the responsibility of teaching his friends about how a child with a disability fits within a family. The success of her teaching in Brian's class led Schmalz to teach about Daniel in her daughter's pre-school group.

In "The Sibling Situation," Betty Pendler responds to a letter from a parent that had been published in *The Exceptional Parent*. She gives details of her straightforward approach to explaining her older daughter's disability to her younger son. She also urges parents to let "our 'normal' children know how we feel inside." In Part III, the younger brother in the article describes his perspective in "Dear Mom."

The article by professionals, which follows the parent-written articles, was co-authored by Helen Stavros and Richard D. Boyd. "But Not Enough to Tell the Truth" is the result of their experiences with workshops for siblings of children with special needs. The workshops, designed to give siblings an opportunity to express themselves, present typical issues and discuss how the children can deal with them. The article provides helpful guidelines for parents about the value of modeling by adults as well as explaining to children that parents can get upset and may behave in ways they wish were different. The authors also remind us that knowing what is "right" may not affect actual behavior.

For the Love of Wess

Victoria Leclerc Therrien

Awakening from a sound sleep, I realized that something was wrong. I could not possibly be in labor; it was a month and a half too early. Early or not, on November 9, 1976, Nathan was born. As proud parents, we admired the five-pound, red, wrinkled body basking under the jaundice lamp. His little head donned the necessary goggles, giving him the appearance of a test pilot ready for action. As we gazed at him, our thoughts drifted off to his future and how happy we were knowing that we would be a part of it.

UNEXPECTED EVENTS

His early birth and jaundice were just the beginning of unexpected events in our lives. As a new mother, I did not find it unusual to be up all hours of the day and night trying to get Nathan to eat. After all, he was a preemie.

During those long hours, though, I began to reflect upon the events immediately after Nathan's birth. What did that nurse mean when she said he was "special?" What was the doctor inferring when he said that there was something wrong with his hips? Why was it necessary to have special testing?

After almost three months of subtle hints and waiting, the head of genetics informed us that Nathan had been diagnosed as having Down syndrome. The term was unfamiliar to both of us. When he explained it meant mongoloid, I broke down in tears. My husband Bob turned to me with questions in his eyes as I searched my memory for clues. Would Nathan be retarded and have a large head?

I was thinking about an article I had read as a college student which concluded that since people with mental retardation have no place in society, they should not exist. I had a sick, guilty feeling remembering that I had passively agreed with the author's position. I also recalled tossing out college notes on a course I had taken about disability, thinking "I will never need these. It could never happen to me." How I wished I had kept them.

Bob and I soon realized that being parents of a child with Down syndrome would be full of difficult challenges. We were fortunate to have a caring pediatrician who did not shock us with the truth of Nathan's disability at birth. After giving us the time to grow to love Nathan, the doctor followed through with the necessary information and guidance. In time, we learned that our handsome little guy with a "normal" sized head would progress slowly but nicely.

WESS

Three years later, we traveled the same long highway to the testing center again. We went for an amniocentesis test to determine whether the second child I was carrying would also be born with Down syndrome. We had not planned this child and, fortunately, the little baby I saw wiggling on the screen during the test was to be a "normal" little boy.

Wess is four now. He is the reason for this article. Ever since conception, his rights have, in a sense, been neglected. His life was threatened at the time of the amniocentesis because we signed a paper stating that the hospital was not responsible for any damage that might occur to the fetus during testing. It was also possible that, as parents, we might have chosen abortion only to find out later that it was a normal fetus.

Even after his birth, I penalized Wess for being normal. As he grew, Nathan continued to be our major concern. We attended all the workshops available to parents of disabled children, including a sign language class to help Nathan learn to talk. We bought expensive special shoes to help him walk more easily and made medical appointments to take care of his eyesight and make sure his teeth would come in straight. Our attention was constantly focused on helping Nathan to learn and play. We were determined he would achieve to his fullest. How could he not? We had put so much time and effort into it. Until last August that is.

BREAKING THE SILENCE

That was when I enrolled in a course for my Master's Degree in education called "Exceptional Children." I intended to acquire as much knowledge about children with mental retardation and programs available to them as I could. The class helped me to understand how individuals with disabilities have been viewed by society historically. I had a grateful feeling knowing that Nathan had been born during a period when so many programs were being provided for exceptional children and their families.

While scanning a journal for a course assignment, a title jumped off the page at me—"The Counseling Needs of Siblings of Mentally Retarded Children." What's this? Siblings have needs? As I read the article, I felt a pang of guilt creep slowly through my body. But it was not until that guilt finally reached my heart that I realized what I had been doing. I was expending all my time and energies on Nathan, figuring that Wess would do all right. After all, he was normal. But was he? Would he be?

I swallowed my concerns until I registered for a research course necessary to complete my Master's Degree. After consulting special educators, I learned that volumes have been written on mental retardation, but little was known about how siblings were affected. After prayerful decision making, I finally had my topic.

It was frustrating to find that many of the books and articles I needed to do my research could not be located locally. So I did some investigating on my own. After exorbitant phone and postage bills, I confirmed the fact that few people had considered the needs of siblings.

Most agencies serving children with disabilities were only concerned with meeting immediate needs. Parents were included in the programs, but siblings were rarely considered. I was fortunate to speak with someone who knew of a sibling program in Wisconsin. It was my first real lead. Later, I located a nurse who worked with sibling groups in Massachusetts. Then I received a letter listing a *Network Newsletter* for siblings as a source of information. At last I was breaking through.

The research was only the beginning. I kept thinking, "How could this help Wess?" I decided to apply my research in a practical direction and prepared a pamphlet entitled, *For The Love of Siblings . . . Who Cope With Special Brothers and Sisters*. The pamphlet addressed "normal" children and their feelings about having disabled siblings. It included suggestions for parents, siblings, and the community at large and listed books and other resources.

I wondered how other parents would react to the pamphlet. I reflected back to my first thoughts that Wess would be negatively affected by Nathan.

It was comforting to know that he could be positively affected as well. I remember the relief I felt after interviewing adult siblings who shared feelings of guilt, shame, grief, denial, resentment, and hostility. Through their experiences, their lives had become richer and more meaningful as they expressed their genuine love for their disabled siblings. They felt their greatest need had been for information. Like parents, they wondered why it had happened to their family and what it would mean for their life.

WESS AND NATHAN

Even though Wess is young, he knows that he is different from his big brother. He often translates for me when Nathan's speech is unclear and willingly helps Nathan with a jacket zipper. He realizes that his brother has difficulty with fine motor skills. We wonder about Wess acting like a big brother when he is really the youngest child.

Perhaps Wess' constant desire to dress as a cowboy, soldier, or superman makes him feel more invincible against the fear of "catching Nathan's disability." Constantly looking in the mirror may be a way of checking his own body to find out whether he is disabled himself. I try to be patient as Wess mimics Nathan's speech and behavior as if he were trying to understand what mental retardation is and whether he could deal with it if it happened to him.

OUR JOB AS PARENTS

I believe it is the job of parents to supply the necessary information so that children will not fear "catching the disability." Puppets and drawings can be used to help a child express what he or she likes and dislikes about his or her disabled sibling. Books are also an excellent tool, giving children the freedom to stare at people with disabilities and ask questions.

My husband and I have given Wess this information in small doses. We have told him that Nathan's disability means he will learn slowly. As Wess gets older, we will discuss his questions about peer relationships, marriage, whether his children will be normal, and what his responsibilities will be toward his brother. Most likely, many years will pass before he fully understands why his brother "couldn't help it," why he was expected to be a model child, why attention from his parents was rationed.

As parents, we realize that we are not only sources of information, but models. If we treat Nathan with patience, love, and understanding, then hopefully Wess will too.

Hopefully, Wess can focus on Nathan's strengths, as we have. We have taken Wess to Nathan's school, therapeutic swim class, and other activities so that he can interact with other families with disabled children and realize that he is not alone.

When Wess enters school, he may feel embarrassed and stigmatized by peers who think that he is different too. In anticipation of that day, we encourage neighborhood children to play in our yard so that they will learn to accept and grow with Nathan. At times, Wess will bravely protect Nathan by saying, "This is my brother and you leave him alone." At other times, he feels compelled to follow those who tease, trick, or always make Nathan the monster. Wess may feel guilty when he doesn't stick up for his brother, or when he bats a ball easily while Nathan tries with little success.

Siblings often feel jealous when parents favor the special brother or sister. Resentment may arise if siblings miss out on college or other activities because of the financial burden placed on the family of a child with a disability.

Resentment may turn into anger when a sibling is made constant guardian of the disabled child or if there are unfair discipline practices. We are careful in giving Wess and Nathan equal amounts of consideration. Wess used to get blamed too quickly when arguments would arise. "Let Nathan have the toy if he wants it"; "Ignore the behavior and he will not do it anymore." What frustration Wess must have felt.

In thinking ahead to Wess' future, I pray that he will have a greater appreciation of his capabilities, be more responsible and patient toward others, and sensitive to prejudice and its consequences.

There are no quick and easy solutions to these and other problems. Each sibling has individual needs. Many of the problems siblings will encounter can be improved with immediate and direct services to the *whole* family with the help of doctors, support groups, special education, group homes, supportive employment, and community awareness. For the love of Wess, will you help by supporting programs to meet the needs of siblings?

A Sibling Born *Without* Disabilities: A Special Kind of Challenge

Paula M. Michalegko

Much has been written about the adjustments we parents must make when we learn our child has a disability. We quickly learn the role we have to play in the child's life and how life will never be the same again. We learn about the stages of acceptance and realize we are constantly moving forward, then regressing, and once more progressing on this scale. We live with "chronic sorrow" and learn to find joy in the simple, everyday facts of the child's life.

When the child with a disability is your only child, he or she becomes "normal" within the home environment. As parents of an only child, there is no basis for comparison until the child is taken outside the home. Upon return, the child is once again "normal" within the family environment.

When a new "normal" sibling is born, everything changes. This is true of a new child in any family but is a special challenge when the older sibling has a disability.

MANY CHANGES

As parents we have to make the most adjustments. Although we now have a healthy, new baby, the structure or balance of the home environment has once again been changed and a variety of adjustments are necessary. Here is our infant who will develop and learn—a child who will walk, talk and may ultimately move beyond the child with a disability. While the prospect of these milestones happening is sheer pleasure to imagine, it is also frightening. After all, no one has written a book for us advising how to cope with this normal child or telling us how we will react emotionally.

When the "normal" sibling comes home, parents are elated, thrilled and cautious, along with a whole host of other emotions. However, few parents would ever stop to think they might encounter some difficulties with their feelings about this child's progress. Sooner or later it happens. The younger sibling grows past the point of development achieved by the child with a disability. Suddenly, the younger brother or sister becomes the "big" brother or sister.

DOUBLE-EDGED SWORD

Without realizing it, the process of parenting this normal child becomes a double-edged sword. We are thrilled and delighted with each accomplishment. It brings us great joy to see this child developing and progressing so well. However, at the same time, the experience can be one of pain—a spark that ignites the flames of chronic sorrow. This is especially true when the normal child surpasses the sibling with a disability. It is a very happy time that can produce, without warning, sadness. As parents, we can ask ourselves: "Why do I feel like this?" "Why can't I see the younger child's accomplishments independent of the older child?" And on and on. It becomes very easy to feel some of the old turmoil, self-doubt and confusion that was felt during the initial stages of coping with a child with a disability. Now here is another child who makes it very difficult for our older child to remain "normal" within the home environment.

SEPARATE BUT EQUAL

My key to the delicate balance needed in such parenting seems to rest on the concept of "separate but equal." As parents, we must continuously bear in mind that each child is unique, an individual unto himself. Like anything, however, it is simple to say or think, but difficult to practice.

Do we come to expect more from the normal child? Are we less tolerant of the shortcomings of that child? Approaching these questions with candor, we would probably have to answer "yes." Of course, this is not true all of the time, or even a majority of the time. Still, we may find ourselves using the child with a disability as a standard to criticize our other child. For example, "You colored that picture well, but if you had tried as hard as your brother does, you could have done better." The sibling will soon get the message that no matter what he or she does, all family life revolves around the child with the disability. The younger child has lost his individuality and has become an extension of the older sibling—the normal part we parents want or wish the older child could have been. It is not always easy for parents to hold these feelings in check and treat each child "separate but equal."

Parents also have the task of developing in the normal child an awareness, respect and concern not only for the sibling with a disability, but for all people with disabilities. We can cultivate these areas by demonstrating them in daily living and by avoiding pampering or preferential treatment of the child with a disability.

All siblings fight and dislike each other during the course of childhood. All siblings dislike a brother or sister intruding when their friends are visiting them. The ultimate goal is for parents to realize these events are acceptable and for siblings to feel parental acceptance of each sibling's perspective. Pushing the younger child to accept his sibling with a disability can only lead to more negative feelings for the younger child.

IT'S NEVER EASY

Parenting in these circumstances can be difficult. Personal awareness, however, can be an essential factor for success. If parents are aware of how they interact individually with the children and together as a family, many potential stumbling blocks can be avoided or lessened in intensity. If we, as parents, allow siblings the same kind of relationships that all siblings have a right to, the development of the family progresses more smoothly.

We all strive to develop a family life that meets our needs and stresses individual growth in each of the children. We want them to develop an awareness that all people are unique and deserving of respect. It is our responsibility to our children to know how we, as adults, feel. We must cope with these feelings before they lead to anger or disappointment. We have to remember that our children are separate and equal, and can only live their own lives and develop their individual characters by the examples we set for them. We must realize that each child can bring joy. There will be times when it is painful enough to deal with a normal child, let alone the child with a disability.

Negative feelings toward our children are part of life. They'll come and go, but they must be acknowledged. We must deal with the negative feelings and grow from them. When we learn to do that, the negative feelings come less often and are shorter in duration.

Parenting is never easy, no matter how ideal the family situation. The development of any healthy family depends on the ability of parents to consider the strengths and weaknesses of each member. This is highlighted when one of the children has a disability. More importantly, parents should realize and remember they are not superhuman. They are entitled to moments of doubt, pain and confusion. In recognizing and coping with these feelings, parents become stronger and, in turn, strengthen the family unit, a structure that requires all members to share their lives on an equal basis.

When the Youngest Becomes the Oldest

Connie E. Post

"Uh oh, uh oh, Thomas is crying," Erika says urgently. She goes to him and tries to find some way to comfort him, but Thomas pushes her away. She looks at me in a curious, somewhat rejected manner. Erika is two and a half years old, and Thomas is four.

Having a child with a disability presents its own difficulties for parents. Add to that the special stresses that siblings of children with special needs go through, and the entire family structure is open to a complex arena of grief, competition, fairness and survival.

THOMAS AND ERIKA

Thomas is our four-year-old who has autism and is mentally retarded. He functions at about a 14 to 18 month level, uses sign language, and can be very enjoyable, as well as very stressful, to be around. Erika is not quite three and is definitely the "older" sibling in our family. She has gone through a unique process in order to deal with Thomas in her own very special way.

Erika's process of dealing with Thomas will continue to grow and develop as the years pass by. For now, as the months pass by, she becomes more of a helper, and she must keep asking me, "Why is Thomas crying?"

and I keep saying, "I don't know." Together, we continue to come up with ways to help Erika deal with her special brother.

FAIRNESS

Unique problems arise when there is a child with a disability in the family. Even the normal sibling issues become exaggerated in our family. For example, the issue of fairness is more difficult. It is hard to make it "fair" when one child demands so much more attention, time and patience.

Sometimes, the normal one gets disciplined for things the child with special needs does not. If Erika yells in the store, she must be told to quiet down. Thomas has no verbal language, but uses lots of noises. If he decides to "get loud" in the store or restaurant, there is really nothing we can do to help him quiet down. His receptive language is so limited, and any verbal explanation does not help. It seems the only thing we can do is leave the area, which we usually are not willing to do. We try to discipline in relation to the needs of each child versus applying the same discipline in all situations.

LANGUAGE EXPECTATIONS

Our language expectations are so different for each child. It is hard for Erika to understand why I tell her to "use words" when she is whining, but I will work with Thomas for 20 minutes when he is whining, trying to figure out what is wrong with him.

It is also difficult for Erika to understand that we have different expectations for neatness concerning food and eating. Thomas' motor problems have forced us to lower our expectations of him to eat neatly. We are coping the best we can, and he is slowly getting there. Erika is much neater except when she is imitating Thomas during mealtime. When she is "messy," it surprises us. She wonders why I put bibs and dishtowels on Thomas during spaghetti-time and do not do the same for her. (Sometimes I just do the same for Erika so she feels as important.)

IMITATION

The first time Erika started spinning around and rolling her eyes back into her head, I almost went nuts. I heard myself starting to tell her not to do that. I thought, "You're not autistic. You don't need to do that." But then I realized that she was merely doing a healthy imitation of her older sibling. It was all she knew.

When she was about two, she started to pull on me (just as Thomas does to communicate with us). At first, I resisted going with her. She is normal. She does not have to communicate this way. It represented too many issues for me. But then I realized that this was her normal. Our family may not be anyone else's normal, but it is our normal. I decided to let her take my hand, and I followed her around for about two weeks. Then slowly, she realized she did not have to communicate that way. But she needed to know I would respond to her in the same way as I did to Thomas, that she was just as important.

REWARDS

It is easy to slip into overzealous rewarding—jumping up and down, doing cartwheels—when the child with a disability does the littlest (biggest) thing. For instance, when Thomas says a word or plays with a toy, we go crazy. We try to always remember that Erika's uniqueness is just as important as Thomas'. We try to acknowledge her accomplishments, no matter how small, as much as we can. It may not always be even, but each one needs to be encouraged and praised. The mere connotation of the phrase "special needs child" implies the opposite of what the normal child needs.

The element of unpredictability sometimes pervades our household. Thomas' skills are so sporadic that it is hard to create some sort of certainty for Erika. Some days he will look at her or accept a toy from her, but it may not happen again for weeks. If Thomas plays with the wagon one day, and Erika says, "He did it, Mommy," it does not mean he will do it again, or that he will build on that skill. It means that Erika must adjust to a lot of ups and downs. As parents, at least we have some adult explanation for this. Erika must "punt," and adjust constantly to things she cannot even comprehend.

SOCIAL EVENTS

Social situations present their own problems for our family. We imagine that in later years, the embarrassment that siblings often feel is going to be addressed. But for now, we must deal with the longing to be a "regular" family at picnics and potlucks.

Thomas looks so normal and is actually very attractive. This may seem like a benefit, but in some ways it is a problem. If a child already "looks" like he has a disability, people lower their expectations for the child's behavior. Having a perfectly normal-looking four-year-old child with very abnormal behavior creates a strange environment of unrealistic expectations and feelings of uncertainty and isolation.

When we go to social gatherings, one parent puts all of his/her energy into watching Thomas. As Thomas gets older and his disability becomes more obvious, social situations may become even more complex. We will always try not to squelch any of Erika's feelings about it. Also, we will try to help her deal with public comments and help her understand that other people's generalizations do not fit our family.

Often, one parent must become Erika's playmate. We play the games with her that Thomas cannot play, and talk about things they cannot discuss together. When we see Erika play so joyfully with her peers without disabilities, we realize how much of a relationship she has lost with Thomas. We try to give her lots of opportunities to play with normal children.

We see Erika feel sad and rejected when Thomas pushes her away. We see her try to make sense of it all when she looks at us and says, "Thomas no talk, Mommy." We see her rejoice in the small interactions Thomas sometimes attempts. Since she is so young, it is difficult to talk extensively about her feelings. We ask her if she feels sad or mad, and sometimes she nods or admits, "I'm mad at Thomas." I think in some way she understands that Thomas just can't do some things. Sometimes I'll say, "Thomas can't use words to tell me he wants juice, so he does sign." Erika has learned a lot of sign language. She has become a part of his learning experience.

FEELINGS

The most important thing we have done and hope to continue doing in our family is to let Erika have her feelings about Thomas. It is the repression of those feelings that will do the harm.

In that same light, we try to help her feel just as important. That may involve doing special things with her. For example, going to the hardware store with Daddy is fun for her. Helping me make brownies or having a friend come over may not be the same as Thomas' attention, but it is special for Erika. We talk about "Thomas' time" when the therapist comes over and "Erika's time" when she gardens with Daddy.

Whenever Thomas starts crying or needs something, Erika is always right there, trying to hug him or figure out what is wrong. When I think it's necessary to let him work it out on his own, I will explain to her that Thomas needs to be alone for awhile. She doesn't like that. She doesn't want to let him cry.

Erika takes on a lot of responsibility for Thomas. To some degree, I think that is necessary. But we try not to force her into the "caretaker" role. Just by her childhood circumstances, Erika may grow up to be a more nurturing person, but I want her to be a child too and not have to always be the caretaker. She is naturally going to take the latter on more readily. In the nursery at my exercise class, she is the one who gets the babies their bottles when they cry and looks for their pacifiers and says, "Oh, what's the matter, baby?" We want to let her be a two-year-old too. We try to help her find a balance.

When Thomas gets into his cycles of hitting, it is very difficult for all of us. When Erika gets hit or pinched, we try to comfort her, instead of giving all the attention to her brother. Sometimes Erika is the one who has done the hitting. Giving the attention to the one who gets hurt seems to have worked. The aggressor does not get a big reaction out of his/her behavior. Sometimes, I will resort to giving Thomas "time out" in his room, since he has a hard time stopping the hitting once it starts.

As time goes on, we will have to advance the complexity of our explanations for Erika about Thomas and why he can't do certain things. In our family, we are trying to foster the idea that everything isn't always fair. We treat our children uniquely, not the same, because they are very different people. They have different needs and we try to meet those, while helping each one to feel important and needed. We allow our family to be different, and to allow what works to work.

Today, Erika runs to me after giving Thomas an animal cracker. "He likes it, Mommy. He likes it!" "That's good, Erika. Does that make you happy?" She nods, "yes," and runs away. Later, Thomas is banging on the window, and she says, "Mommy, Thomas banging." I say, "I know, Erika, I know." We go to get him and then she runs off to watch the rest of "Sesame Street."

Brothers With a Difference

Renee Seidenberg

My son Mark's disability has been called by many names: Infantile Autism in its residual state, Child Development Disorder or Atypical Pervasive Development Disorder (according to the official psychiatric classification), and E.D. or emotionally disturbed (according to the classification with the Committee for the Handicapped and the school system).

Parenting a child with a disability is a lonely business. Sharing the depth of despair would be admitting defeat, so you press it down.

I often get angry at my husband because he only wants to look at, or talk about, the positive sides of Mark. He continually sees progress. His optimism keeps me up, even though I often know that he is far from being realistic.

SHATTERED DREAMS

I will never forget the sound of my dreams shattering when a professional told me that Mark would never be able to go to regular schools. He was only thirty months old at the time. Until then, I had vivid daydreams of my two boys, less than two years apart, walking together to school. They are beautiful, loving, and loved; they are both wanted, enjoyed, nurtured, and spoiled.

When Erik, who is younger, was born, my husband bought me a statue of two young boys hand-in-hand. I still choke up when I look at it and think of what might have been. Then I swallow and hope that maybe next year, Mark will be better.

Mark is a tall, blond, very handsome boy with huge eyes and a big smile. He knew all of his letters at the age of eighteen months and could read well by the age of three. He taught himself by watching Sesame Street. He has a phenomenal memory. A pediatric neurologist labeled him a genius at the age of three and one half.

Still, during Mark's first year in the public school system, everything went wrong. Mark has difficulty communicating and/or relating to his environment. He spends a lot of time either walking in circles, running, or talking to himself. He does not pick up any social cues, and he learns only by imitation. He will remember what to do or say only if we remember to tell him in advance.

His school had to be changed in midyear, and we spent a lot of time just trying to find him a proper school. Like all of us, Erik was affected, although as parents we imagined we could protect him from pain, as if he lived in a vacuum.

WHAT ABOUT ERIK?

I have known for almost two years that Erik was having problems understanding his brother Mark, but we have hardly talked about it. When Erik was four years old and in nursery school, the teacher called me in for a special conference. She nervously showed me some pictures that Erik had drawn of his brother. They were angry pictures, mean and full of self-pity. The words Erik had used to describe the pictures made his pain about having a brother like Mark come through very clearly.

The pictures devastated me. I broke down in tears and remember being engulfed in overwhelming fatigue. I had, I thought, struck a balance between keeping my sons independent and helping them build a positive relationship. For the sake of convenience, I had enrolled them both in the same after-school programs—gym, swimming lessons—and the same summer camp. Mark often exhibits very irritating behaviors, and it is impossible to avoid them. My husband has always felt the shared activities were good, that Erik has to learn to accept and protect his brother. Living with Mark is a reality for Erik, but sometimes I want to shield him from all unnecessary pain and embarrassment. Sometimes, I want to shield myself.

Two summers ago, an acquaintance of mine at our summer club was describing this really strange kid that people were talking about, who was, she said, approximately the same age as one of mine. Her tone was fearful. She did not know it then, but she was describing Mark. I said to her that it sounded like my son, but she insisted it could not be. She knew Mark, and he was not like that. But my friend was wrong! That is how deceiving and disturbing his problems can be. She did eventually realize her mistake, and I am sure felt terrible, but neither of us ever mentioned it again. She has grown used to Mark's behavior and knows that I watch him constantly.

TRYING TO "PROTECT" MY SONS

I have talked at length with other mothers about their non-disabled children. I have found that we struggle with the same problems. How can I protect Erik from his brother's emotional disturbances, yet encourage their friendship? How can I encourage Erik to make his own friends, without worrying that Mark will disrupt their play with emotional outbursts and inappropriate behavior? And, of course, how can I deal with Mark's hurt feelings when he has no one to play with, when Erik has been invited to other children's houses?

As Mark grows older and bigger, his inappropriate behavior is more and more difficult to explain. I have witnessed the painful look in Erik's eyes when we have to leave somewhere quickly because of Mark's emotional outbursts. Recently, in a supermarket, Erik wanted to introduce Mark to a school friend, but Mark could not be brought out of his trance-like behavior. Erik finally shrugged and told his friend that "over there talking to himself is my brother Mark. Don't worry, he does that all the time." I didn't know what to say. I just gave Erik a hug.

Fortunately for us, Erik is a wonderful child. Bringing him up so far has been very easy. He is sweet, bright, and very loving. He walked and talked early and is very popular with his teachers and classmates. Erik's big brother Mark has been reading him stories for years now, looks things up for him in the encyclopedias, knows all about dinosaurs including their difficult names, shows him on different maps or in the *National Geographic* where all different types of animals live, remembers every single name of Transformers that we have, and goes to a special school far from home.

Erik, now in kindergarten, who still cannot read, wants to go to Mark's school so he can learn "faster." To explain the "special" school to Erik, we said that Mark needed a lot of speech therapy to help him communicate better and ease his frustrations. Recently, I heard this long conversation in the back of my car, Erik is telling Mark that he will have go to his "special" school because he couldn't say "mouse" (meaning "mouth" as I found out after probing) and had to see a speech therapist in his school. The sweet irony of this made me laugh even though it was a little sad.

I have no way of knowing if, in his own way, he is trying to make it up to us for his difficult sibling, but if I am able to believe that Mark was born the way he is, then I have to believe that Erik was too.

QUESTIONS FOR THE FUTURE

Should we try to mainstream Mark into the same school system as Erik? There is no question that if Mark could handle it, it would be good for him. It would enable him to be more a part of our community and give him a chance to develop friends. Even just one friend from our neighborhood would be wonderful. But what would that do for Erik? Would he be subjected to cruel teasing and have to be his brother's keeper? Would it harm Erik's development to impose on him a brother who may at times cause him embarrassment? If so, will the benefits for Mark make it worthwhile? Which child is sacrificed?

Having a "different" child constantly shakes your faith in your parenting skills. There are some parents' groups (mostly mothers' groups) in the different associations that I belong to, and it does help to share the pain, but there are few resources for the siblings of our disabled children. They too need the chance to ventilate their own pain and frustrations.

Darwin and Caleb

Susanne Carter

When our son was three years old we were to become parents for the second time. An amniocentesis showed that we were to have a "normal," male child. We did not know what to expect from this newest member of our family. We had become accustomed to wading through the jungle of paperwork that is a required companion of special education; we were used to searching for those rare boxes of extra-large diapers most normal children who are toilet-trained on schedule never need; and we had become comfortable in answering children in the grocery store who would stare at Darwin babbling to himself and inquire, "Is he a baby?"

Naturally, we had read the textbooks that outlined what developmental milestones could be expected and when to expect them for a normally developing child. I had read them during my first pregnancy and then had packed them away as too depressing after Darwin's birth, when it became evident that he would never keep pace with what is considered normal. After Caleb's birth, I dug out those child development books once more, this time in anticipation of sharing each step with him.

Now at the age of two, Caleb already talks in sentences, builds block houses, knows the alphabet, and sings "Twinkle, Twinkle Little Star" (off key). These are accomplishments we will never take for granted, for we know that realistically, our moderate-to-severely retarded son will never be able to articulate well enough to talk in sentences or be creative enough to build a block house.

But the coming of Caleb into our family has brought me much more than the satisfaction of watching a child develop as Dr. Spock predicted he should. Caleb, unknowingly, has brought about a significant change in my relationship with my oldest son.

WHEN DARWIN WAS BORN . . .

Darwin was born five years ago with Down syndrome. At the time I was thirty-two years old. The odds of having a child with an extra chromosome at that age are 1000 to 1. I thought that the fact that I ate wheat germ and broccoli and drank nothing stronger than orange juice would ensure that my odds were even greater against having a child with a problem.

But nature sometimes errs without explanation and Darwin was given an extra chromosome at conception. My husband and I were told of his disability the day after he was born. We vowed not to waste our time grieving for the normal son we had lost. We channeled our energies into loving and stimulating Darwin as much as we could, helping him to develop whatever potential he had.

EARLY INTERVENTION

We enrolled Darwin in an infant stimulation class at the local school for children with disabilities. I took him twice a week until he "graduated" into the daily program when he was eighteen months old. We also arranged for Darwin to have speech therapy. We hired special education majors from a local university to work with him after school until we got home from work. And at night and on weekends we worked puzzles, built towers, threw balls, read books, did exercises, played music—everything we could think of to stimulate Darwin's mental and physical growth.

Darwin did progress, but most of his achievements came at an extremely slow pace and after much work. We taught him to crawl by physically maneuvering his arms and legs, me at his head and his father at his feet. A friend gave him a toy typewriter for his first birthday. It was not until his second birthday that he was able to press down the keys without assistance.

RISKS OF A SECOND PREGNANCY

We never intended to have only one child. However, having given birth to one child with a chromosomal abnormality increased our chances to 1 in

100 of having another child with a similar disability. At Darwin's school I had been introduced to a host of various syndromes, disabilities, and conditions I never knew existed. I knew having a second child was taking a risk. Could we handle another child? What if a new baby had a second set of problems to deal with—problems which might even be more severe than Darwin's?

Yet many childhood experiences are meant to be shared, and having a brother or sister to share them with makes them much more enjoyable. Riding in a wagon, splashing in the bathtub, eating ice cream cones, building castles in the sand—so many childhood experiences seem meant for two.

We also knew that if we never took the risk of having another child, Darwin would grow up alone without someone to join him splashing in the bathtub or eating ice cream cones, and we might never experience the joy of watching a normal child develop. We would also pass up the opportunity for Darwin to have a normal sibling role model and for us to have a child who might be patient enough to want to help his brother when he grew older.

A NEW OUTLOOK

As we have witnessed Caleb developing very close to the way textbooks outline normal development, we have often looked at each other in amazement at the things he remembers, not only his address but his best friend's as well; the things he says, when he was twenty-two months old and sorting out differences between male and female, he greeted me at the door one day with, "Hi, woman!"; and the things he does, putting together 25-piece jigsaw puzzles with little help. However, we did not foresee two very unexpected contributions Caleb has made to our family. First, he has helped me to relax and enjoy Darwin more for the individual that he is. And, he has helped me to appreciate some of Darwin's attributes I may have otherwise taken for granted.

Before Caleb was born, I read book after book about child development and how-to manuals on working with children who were mentally retarded. I knew every skill Darwin should be attaining at each age level but was not. I had the mistaken belief that there was a direct correlation between the time I spent working with Darwin and his ability to keep progressing. On days he "worked" well I felt a sense of accomplishment; on days when he would not stack his blocks or refused to scribble with a crayon, two items which ALWAYS appear on developmental evaluations, I felt a sense of defeat. I felt compelled to spend most of my time at home working with him. It was only when he was asleep that I would allow myself to relax. Often I felt exhausted.

OBSERVING THEIR DIFFERENCES

The first major difference I noticed between Darwin and Caleb (besides phenotypes—Darwin is short and squatty; Caleb is lean and tall) was Caleb's awareness as an infant. Perched in his infant seat, he seemed to scrutinize our every move. And when he was old enough to begin vocalizing he started to point to everything, hungry to know "What's that?" We would label an object for him once and he would carefully tuck it away in his information retrieval system until he needed to utilize it later. I began to realize that Caleb was absorbing information as a very natural part of his daily routine. With Darwin "absorbing" meant months and months of drill work.

I nearly panicked the first time Caleb picked up a fistful of rocks and then stuffed them into his mouth, like a ravenous chipmunk. I assumed he was going to eat them; but after this happened repeatedly with no rocks swallowed I realized with relief that Caleb was simply learning about the texture of rocks by feeling them in his mouth.

Every time it snows Caleb wants to climb up on a chair and watch the flakes fall. He is fascinated by the fluffy covering on the sidewalk which can be magically rolled up into big balls and shaped to look like a person! But to Darwin snow is just a hindrance. It makes his awkward walking gait even more unsteady and its cloddiness stuns him.

Through observing the differences between Darwin and Caleb at an early age I came to realize that the most important ingredients a child needs in order to learn are awareness and curiosity—two traits Darwin rarely displays. This realization did not sadden me. Instead, it came as a relief, for it also came as an explanation for why Darwin was not progressing as much as I expected he would, despite my diligence.

REALISTIC EXPECTATIONS

As my expectations for Darwin became more realistic I began to spend less time trying to work with him and more time actually playing with him, doing the kinds of things he most enjoys—dancing to music, splashing in the water, swinging, and roughhousing. I have not stopped working with Darwin but neither do I attack his IEP (Individualized Educational Plan) like some variation of Don Quixote fighting windmills. And if he has a bad day at the "office," well, so do we all; I do not take it personally. When Darwin will not stack more than three blocks I can recall the day he stacked thirteen. When he cannot remember his body parts today, I remember him pointing correctly to all of them yesterday and hope that he will remember tomorrow.

Darwin, like retarded children, has "obsessions." I assumed this characteristic was unique among the mentally retarded until last Christmas when Caleb received several books with pictures of animals in them from his grandparents. For some inexplicable reason he became enthralled with a picture of an ugly, warty, pop-eyed, giant toad. And whenever he went to the bookcase and selected that particular book he would turn to the page with the ugly, warty, pop-eyed, giant toad and refuse to budge.

Later came "obsessions" with cars and trucks, motorcycles, and lawn mowers—anything that made noise and moved simultaneously. These obsessions have made it easier for me to accept Darwin's own special brand of obsessions. Darwin tends to become attached to more unusual things—hoses, vacuum cleaner brushes, light switches—and they sometimes lead to rather bizarre behaviors (he's been known to get up at 3 a.m. and give light shows) but these obsessions pass, as do most childhood phases.

From Darwin and Caleb I have learned that not all normal patterns of behavior are necessarily positive and not all abnormal behaviors are necessarily negative. Having Caleb has helped me to appreciate some of Darwin's special qualities that may not be normal but nevertheless make him more endearing to us.

Caleb, just entering the "terrible two" stage, often becomes emotionally "charged," especially when tired or hungry, and he will resort to biting, kicking, hitting, and pushing in order to work out his frustrations—just what most normal two-year-olds do. Darwin, on the other hand, has never been through the "terrible twos." The thought of striking someone would never occur to him; he specializes in hugs. Many times he's a much easier child to love because he does not have the mood swings that make Caleb quite unpredictable at times.

Caleb's normal dose of impatience has helped me to appreciate Darwin's often large reserves of patience. When we are traveling in the car, Caleb will tolerate sitting in his car seat for a maximum of thirty minutes. Then, without the bribe of a sucker or something at least as enticing, he is ready to GET OUT. If Darwin, on the other hand, has his favorite rock music playing on the tape recorder, he will sit back, mellow out, and contentedly ride for miles and miles. I never realized what a good traveler Darwin was until I had to deal with Houdini in the back seat!

Caleb's awareness sometimes works as a detriment, especially in the grocery store. While Darwin enjoys the ride in the shopping cart, and only occasionally decides to sneak a cookie to eat before it is paid for, Caleb spies the Big Bird bubble bath, the five for $1 cars that fall apart in twenty minutes, and the $3.99 blueberry cheesecake ice cream we cannot afford. It is a challenge to keep him in the grocery cart seat and still succeed in purchasing everything on our grocery list.

Darwin is very slow and methodical in eating. We did not realize what an advantage this was until Caleb was old enough to take out to eat with us. We usually go to Burger King because "ergers" are Darwin's favorite meal. Caleb is so excited about the environment (the whirling ceiling fans, the crowns on kids' heads, the birthday parties in mid-bash, the enticing jungle gym sets outside the window) that he takes two bites of his hamburger and is ready to GET DOWN and explore this fascinating place. Not Darwin. He savors every bite of "erger," every sip of chocolate milk shake, and will gladly offer to clean up the residue from Caleb's plate. The lucky parent gets to enjoy a peaceful meal beside Darwin while the less lucky parent follows the more adventurous and less hungry at the moment, Caleb.

Caleb, at two, is already succumbing to peer pressure. If his friend is wearing Masters of the Universe underwear, then so must he (never mind that he's not toilet trained yet). If Darwin is eating an oatmeal raisin cookie, then Caleb must munch on an oatmeal raisin cookie also.

Darwin, unlike Caleb, will never insist upon wearing underwear with Masters of the Universe across the seat because his friends are wearing them. Nor will he beg for Count Chocula cereal for breakfast because that is what his friends eat. His likes and dislikes are very much his own.

For us, the most difficult part of having a retarded child has been the communication gap. Darwin understands little of what we say to him and his garbled, one-word utterances are often unintelligible to us. We often admit to ourselves that we love Darwin but find it incredibly fun to be able to actually carry on a conversation with Caleb. Yet Darwin has his own special qualities that endear him to us. And having a normal child has helped me to see those more clearly and enjoy my son with Down syndrome just as he is.

Christina Loves Katherine

Katherine Berg

We have two daughters; Katherine is five years old, Christina is seven. Katherine is mentally retarded.

Our friends' most common questions are, "Does Christina play with Katherine? Is Christina jealous of the attention Katherine receives, or embarrassed by her? Do they fight, or does Christina ridicule Katherine?" My husband and I are thrilled that we can answer these questions with one simple phrase, "Christina loves Katherine."

Her love is evident in the spontaneous kiss or hug she gives Katherine as they watch television together. In their bathtub play, as they sing nursery rhymes, Christina slows down to let Katherine catch up. Christina also lets Katherine dress in her outgrown ballet shoes and dresses, and they pirouette together to music.

This affection between two sisters has developed naturally, and continues to grow stronger. Of course there are moments when Katherine irritates Christina. If Katherine pulls books out of her sister's bookcase, messing up the room she has just cleaned, Christina becomes furious. Who wouldn't?

But Christina's pervading attitude towards her retarded sister is one of fondness and acceptance. Parents who experience more than "normal" conflict between their disabled child and his siblings may wonder how we did this. Why aren't our family relationships less chaotic, they wonder. I would like to mention several points that have helped us as a family.

PARENTS AS MODELS

It is important that the parents acknowledge to themselves that their child is disabled. Then parents need to be genuine in their acceptance and love for their child. Children copy their parents' behavior; if a father kicks a dog, his children will also. If a mother ignores a disabled child, his brothers will also.

My husband and I share the same amounts of time with our retarded child and our normal child. We read to Katherine, ask her questions about school (which she cannot answer easily), roughhouse with her. We find that Christina does all this with Katherine when we are busy. Christina senses that we love Katherine and that she is important. Christina adopts this attitude also.

EXPLANATION AIDS UNDERSTANDING

As parents you need to tell your children that they have a disabled sibling. Young children have difficulty grasping the meaning of mental retardation or other technical terms. But a child 4 or 5 years old begins to understand how a disabled brother or sister is different from other children.

For instance, Christina can see that Katherine walks and runs awkwardly. She hears Katherine mispronounce words. Her simple phrases are jumbled, like a 3 year old, and she uses gestures frequently. My husband and I try to help Christina understand these different characteristics her retarded sister has. We have simply said, "Katherine will develop more slowly than other children. But she likes to play with toys and friends, like any child does." As Christina has other questions, we answer them clearly and simply. For instance, when Katherine turned 5, Christina said, "Now she can go to my old kindergarten, Mommy." But we explained that Katherine would stay at the training center for retarded children, because she learned more slowly and she liked her teacher (who was specially trained to work with retarded children).

MEET OTHER CHILDREN

Take your normal children to visit your disabled child's class. And emphasize the positive characteristics of the children you see. Christina saw other children, more severely and less severely retarded than her sister. When Christina visited Katherine's class I pointed out, "That's Naomi, doesn't she have a pretty smile. And look at Chris, he thinks he is a cowboy. He looks so proud and happy." Christina boasts to her friends about

Katherine's long, naturally curly hair, how pretty she looks in pink dresses, and how well she claps and dances to her records.

TIME FOR THEMSELVES

Do not demand that your other children play with their disabled sibling all the time. Your other children must have their own friends and be able to play with them alone. I usually ask Christina and her friends to play with Katherine a half hour after school. Then I call Katherine to the kitchen to help me, and let Christina play games with her friends that she could not do with a bratty sister around.

CHILDREN CAN HELP

Parents can encourage their other children to help teach their disabled sibling. Christina often teaches Katherine to cut, or color, or she says, "Now repeat, Row, Row, Row your Boat, after me, Katherine." Christina praises Katherine warmly after her efforts.

LAW AND ORDER

Finally, parents need to be strict with their disabled child, and not spoil him or let him tyrannize and upset the household. Then siblings have the right to become angry.

All disabled children and adults need and deserve to be loved by their parents and brothers and sisters. Only then will other children and adults in the community share this love and friendliness for disabled people.

When Christina was six years old, she said to me one night before going to sleep, "Mommy, black people and retarded people are more alike than anyone else. They know what it's like not to be liked by white people."

Is That Your Brother?
Our Family's Response

Nancy Schmalz

Beaming with pride, the first-grade actors in their construction-paper costumes basked briefly in their parents' applause, then tumbled from their makeshift stage into the audience. I joined in congratulating my son Brian and his classmates, enjoying the reflected warmth of accomplishment shared now by the children and their families. As the first-graders lined up to return to their classroom, one of them pointed to the stroller in which my other son, five-year-old Daniel, was sitting, and directed a question at Brian: "Is that your brother?"

It was undoubtedly an innocent question, but as I glanced at Daniel, curled up and drooling, his long skinny legs sticking out awkwardly from the oversized stroller, I instinctively bristled and wondered how Brian would respond.

PART OF OUR FAMILY

Whether he was still floating in the clouds of his stage success, or whether he was as yet unaware of negative attitudes toward disabled persons, he did not hear the inference I had imagined. Tousling Daniel's hair affectionately with one hand, and corralling his three-year-old sister Heidi with the other, he answered with a toothless grin, "Yes, and this is my sister."

This incident was quickly lost in the mesh of daily events which followed, but I thought about it often, until its significance became clear to me. We had been extremely fortunate that in all of Daniel's five years, we had experienced only positive reactions toward him, from grandparents, teachers, and friends. Even strangers in the grocery store were more likely to say sympathetically, "The little guy's tired today," than to stare or whisper about Daniel's floppy limbs and unsmiling face. Because Brian was only two when Daniel was born, he did not have expectations of a chattering lively playmate, so he accepted each of Daniel's problems in turn as part of the adventure of having a baby brother. By the time it became apparent that Daniel would not be like other babies, he was so thoroughly a part of the family that Brian just continued loving him the way he was.

I knew, however, that this idyllic situation could not last. Brian would shortly need to have answers for his friends' questions and I felt a responsibility to prepare him to deal with their observations in a rational and understanding way. I hoped also to make him aware that he had the responsibility to share with his friends what he had learned from Daniel about persons who have disabilities and the way they fit into a family.

TEACHING MY SON'S FRIENDS

The opportunity to do something about my resolution presented itself the next fall when Brian and his classmates, now second graders, were having a party for which I provided some of the refreshments. As Daniel, Heidi and I delivered the box of goodies that afternoon, unspoken questions filled the room; the queries which were expressed were timidly beside the point: "How old is he?" "What is his name?" I arranged with Brian's teacher to return the next week so that I could introduce Daniel to the class.

As I prepared for my visit with the second graders, I tried to clarify my reasons for going and the goals I hoped to achieve. The most important purpose, I thought, was to help the children realize that Brian and I were happy to talk about Daniel, so that they wouldn't feel embarrassed or guilty about their questions. I wanted them to understand that their observations were part of whatever else they were learning in health and social science: retardation and physical disability are not subjects which must be discussed quietly, soberly, or in private.

Secondly, I planned to demonstrate for the children the great similarities between their own lives and Daniel's. They were interested to know that he goes to school, that he is very fond of ice cream, and that he enjoys going for walks. Brian's teacher provided an appropriate introduction to our discussion by asking questions which helped the children think about individual differences and similarities, among class members and within the community.

My final point concerned our family and the way Daniel and Brian fit into it. I tried to anticipate the questions which classmates might ask Brian and to give simple, factual, unemotional answers. We discussed the ways in which Brian helps with Daniel's care and I gave Brian the opportunity to explain some of the special knowledge that he had gained by working with Daniel.

The entire session lasted about twenty minutes and became a free-for-all discussion of the children's own experiences with disabled individuals and their suggestions for appropriate ways to help a disabled person. By the time the class was dismissed, Daniel was no longer the focal point, though many of the children spoke briefly to him as they left. I sensed that they accepted him as another child rather than as a curiosity.

TEACHING YOUNGER CHILDREN TOO

Encouraged by the responses of the seven-year-olds to ideas which I did not begin to think about until Daniel was born, I wondered about younger children's perceptions of disabled peers. Heidi was attending a child care center a few hours a week, so I listened to the children's reactions when Daniel and I came to pick her up. Refreshingly uninhibited, the three-year-olds' comments reflected their own honest view of things, unrefined by adult taboos and biases. Many of them wondered aloud why such a big boy was riding in a stroller. I responded that he used the stroller because he doesn't walk and he is too big to carry.

I had overheard a well-meaning staff member explain to a little girl that Daniel needs a stroller because "he is special." In my opinion, such an answer, while intended to teach feelings of compassion and open-mindedness, could easily generate a flood of confusion in the mind of a three-year-old. "Is he special because he rides in a stroller?" "Is he especially good or especially bad?" "Am I special too?" "Do I want to be called special?" Better, I think, to give the unadorned truth and let the children learn compassion and tolerance by observing these attitudes in action.

When I asked the director of the child care center if I could bring Daniel for a short visit with Heidi's class, she immediately agreed, and said that I could also meet with the four and five-year-olds. So, the next week Daniel and I joined the circle of children on the floor. My intent was simply to show Heidi's friends that their observations about Daniel's differences were correct, but that he was also very much like them, or like babies they knew. They were interested in the skills which Daniel is learning at school; they rolled over on the floor and hung tightly onto my fingers themselves, then put their little fingers into Daniel's hand to feel his gentle grasp, as they remembered how long ago they had learned to do that. I wanted to show them also that Daniel's need for affection is just like theirs. I invited them to help me hold him and had so many volunteers that they needed to take turns.

The older children asked thoughtful questions about why Daniel couldn't walk, and whether he could see and hear, and whether someday he would smile. I answered these truthfully by saying that we have no answers for some questions about Daniel. I pointed out that we continue to learn more about Daniel and about all children every day. I think it would be as false to invent answers where there are none as to withhold information which could be helpful, and the idea of unsolved mysteries was surely not new to these children.

After our visits with the child care classes I noticed several positive changes. Instead of backing out of our way when I wheeled Daniel's stroller through the room, the other children asked if they could push him. I heard echoes of the visit we had, little children explaining to each other and to me that Daniel uses a stroller because he does not walk, and that he likes ice cream too. The most convincing proof of the success of our experiment was Heidi's repeated request that we do it again, because she liked it when her friends held Daniel.

TEACHING AND LEARNING TOGETHER

These three events, shared with my own and other children, have been deep learning experiences for me. I hope that they can be helpful to other mothers who are searching for a way to help siblings deal with a disabled brother or sister. I realize that it is too early to say that everyone in these stories lived happily ever after, for Daniel is changing, as are the rest of us, and there will undoubtedly be some stormy days along with the sunny ones. It is my belief, however, that young children have a great capacity for appreciating other people. Their natural optimism and freedom from learned bias are assets which can be used to great advantage in situations like those I have described. Early positive experiences with disabled peers seem to be the most effective way to help children begin to understand that difference exists only relative to similarity, and that contributions of individuals may take many, equally valuable forms.

The Sibling Situation

Betty Pendler

I want to respond to Mrs. J. Bowes, Chicago, Illinois, who, in your Oct/Nov/Dec issue, asked about how other parents handle the sibling situation. I won't even use the word "problem," because I firmly believe if the parents do not consider it a problem, then it will never be one. By that I wish to say that there is no question in my mind that the parents set the stage for the way the siblings, the neighbors and the community will view the child.

I am the mother of a girl with Down syndrome. Early in my soul searching development, I decided that I would act "as if" she were normal (without losing sight of reality) and consciously treat her as a child first, who happened to be retarded. However, I very openly talked about her retardation, even to her younger brother as early as age three. So please, Mrs. Bowes, do not think that your nine and five-year-olds are too young to understand. They may not get the conceptual meaning of *mentally retarded*, but you must not be afraid to use the term openly and freely to anyone, with the view that having a mentally retarded sibling is just another fact of life that the family constellation has to live with without making it an earth shaking experience.

As early as age four, my son Paul asked about why his sister Lisa talked funny. I explained, without knowing how much of it he was absorbing, that just as some people are born with one leg and can't walk or others can't hear well, so Lisa was born with a smaller brain and was retarded. She couldn't speak or learn as well but she was a wonderful sister in spite of it.

Then the good old television came to my aid quite unexpectedly. We were all watching "Lassie." The boy asked his mother if Lassie could catch beavers. When told that she couldn't, the little boy had a very crestfallen look on his face. Then his mother said, "But dear, even though Lassie can't catch beavers she has her own special value." The little boy agreed and smiled broadly. I latched on to that phrase and immediately said to my son: "You see, that is like your sister Lisa; even though she doesn't speak well, she has her own special value."

I had no idea if he knew what I was talking about until the following summer when we were all at a family sleep-away camp. One morning, I overheard the next door young camper say to Paul, "Your sister talks funny." Paul replied, "Yes, but don't you know she is like Lassie—she has her own special value." This was at age six. I am happy to say that this groundwork has yielded excellent results.

The second important thing I did, when he was a bit older (around ten), was to speak very openly about his inner feelings towards having a sister who was different. I let him know that I knew it wasn't easy. I urged him to talk freely about it in the same manner that I was doing. To my delight, he reported back to me that he spoke up in his hygiene class when they talked about chromosomes. It turned out that two of his classmates had siblings or relatives who were retarded.

I have found that the questions and comments should be brought out in the open. Our "normal" children should know how we feel inside—our heartbreak and our frustrations at bringing up a different child. Then they know that their secret thoughts are not unique. I always encouraged Paul to invite his friends over but suggested that if he felt uncomfortable having Lisa around, I would arrange for her to be out. But once again, because he was brought up to know that Lisa's condition was not his fault, my fault or her fault, he felt free to have his friends visit. In fact, I have overheard him displaying a sense of pride at her accomplishments, as he explained to his friend, "even though she can't speak or do things as well as we can she sure has her special value."

I knew I had succeeded in my effort to have him feel comfortable with a sister who is different, when he began to take guitar lessons (at age twelve) and made up some of his own songs, including the following:

> I know a girl named Lisa Pendler
> I know her because she's my sister
> She's mentally retarded, but I don't give a darn because—

CHORUS:

She can play like the other girls can
She can sing like the other girls can
She can laugh like the other girls can
And most of all, she can be loved
Like the other girls can.

Let me tell you a story
What some people say
They say she's different from everyone else
But I know differently, because—

(chorus)

Let me tell you another story
One day she's very happy
The next day she is very sad
I know that all girls are like that so
She's not different from anyone because
She can sing like the other girls can
She can play like the other girls can
She can laugh like the other girls
and most of all
She can be loved like the other girls can.

It works, Mrs. Bowes. The combination of emphasizing the positive values, along with free and open conversations with your children. And letting them know that it isn't easy for you either. Good luck.

But Not Enough to Tell the Truth: Developmental Needs of Siblings

Helen Stavros and Richard D. Boyd

"Sometimes," offered Jenifer, "when I've done something that I know my parents are gonna yell at me for, I tell them Randy did it. Like when I forgot to flush the toilet and Dad yelled 'who forgot to flush the toilet!' I told him Randy did it. Then I went into my brother's room and told him what I had done. I felt guilty."

"Yeah," agreed Nicole, "that's like the time I broke the cookie jar in the kitchen. When Mom started yelling, I told her Jason did it. I felt guilty, but not enough to tell the truth."

Jenifer is a 10-year-old girl who has a twin brother, Randy, with Down syndrome. Randy has few verbal skills and frequently creates situations that are embarrassing for his three siblings, who are close in age.

Nicole, also 10, has a three-year-old brother with Down syndrome. While Nicole's brother has not yet embarrassed her through his behavior, Nicole finds it difficult to tell her friends and neighbors about his condition.

Nicole and Jenifer, along with four other children aged eight to twelve, had participated in a four-session workshop for siblings of children with special needs. The workshop was designed to help siblings express their feelings and concerns, and learn how to handle common, yet thorny situations. The children's parents participated in a separate group held concurrently.

The meetings covered material presented in the *Sibshop Manual* developed at the University of Washington, and in the book *Living with a Brother or Sister with Special Needs*. In particular, common conflict and problem situations that siblings might encounter were presented, and the children were asked how they would handle them. Time was also allotted to discuss disabling conditions, special education and simple behavior management principles.

The children expressed many feelings about their siblings with disabilities through role play, group discussion and sharing family stories. When asked to describe typical feelings, virtually all of the children listed embarrassment, pride and jealousy: embarrassment when they came into contact with the world outside the family, pride when their sibling learned something new, and jealousy when their parents spent a disproportionate amount of time with their sibling with a disability. Envy was also mentioned by some whenever a sibling with a disability had little or no homework, few household responsibilities and fewer expectations placed on them by the parents.

The children proved to be knowledgeable and aware of what it means to have a sibling with a disability, benefitting from having open and informed parents. Yet it became apparent that these bright and forthright kids had great difficulty translating knowledge into appropriate and effective action. Their reactions were often based more on the feelings aroused by a situation than on what they knew to be the best response.

One 10-year-old girl, for example, told how she was unable to control her temper when her brother waved his hands in front of her face, even though she could clearly state that ignoring him was the best response. Others knew how to explain to friends or strangers that their brother or sister was disabled, but confessed that their performance broke down when they became embarrassed or angered by the ignorance and insensitivity of others. And one eight-year-old girl explained away her brother's delayed development by telling people he has a hole in his heart, even though she knew she was not being completely honest in doing so.

This gap between the knowing and the doing presents an interesting challenge for non-disabled children and their parents. As the children in this group clearly articulated, they felt guilty whenever they failed to respond in the way they knew to be best. Their parents, in turn, often became frustrated when they saw their non-disabled children "falling short." Yet it would be easy and foolish for parents to vent anger at the non-disabled child, as this would only increase that child's sense of guilt, foster resentment toward the sibling with a disability, and deny them the support and understanding they need to become more assertive.

Children in the preteen years commonly lack the ability to assert themselves, having been trained most of their lives to respect authority and avoid conflict. Those parents who recognize and understand the implications of this developmental stage will be in a better position to help their children become more assertive.

While non-disabled children need to know how to handle certain situations, they also need understanding from adults who can provide a forum for discussing what goes wrong and how to behave differently. Workshops provide one such forum, but the best and most enduring forum is created by open, honest and caring parents.

What can parents do to serve the needs of all their children? While any answer must, ultimately, depend upon individual circumstances, here are some guidelines that can prove helpful:

- Be sure that your expectations for your non-disabled child are realistic. It's easy to forget, sometimes, that they are children first, and we cannot expect them to handle difficult situations like little adults. For example, it would be unrealistic to expect a young child to be able to supervise, alone, a disruptive sibling while in public.

- Let your child know that you also get upset sometimes and often wish you could have been more assertive in a particular situation. Sharing an account of your own shortcomings can ease the sense of shame and guilt that the non-disabled child might feel over some incident of his own.

- Praise your child whenever she's done something of which you want to see more. Let her know specifically what it was that you liked, such as saying, "I liked the way you played with your brother today while I was fixing dinner."

- Don't expect too much too soon. Progress often comes in short, sometimes halting steps. Neither should you be surprised by occasional setbacks, being sure to give corrections in a gentle, positive manner.

- Keep the lines of communication open, paying attention to the feelings underlying what your child tells you. Let him know that his observations, concerns and suggestions are valued and worthy of discussion.

- Remember that the non-disabled sibling will have occasional negative feelings toward the child with a disability and that these feelings are normal and best approached with understanding and not with shame or guilt.

- Most importantly, show your child how you want him or her to behave. There is no substitute for a positive example, especially when it is coupled with the opportunity to practice appropriate behavior under the watchful eye of a warm, supportive parent.

- Finally, help establish a sibling program in your community by encouraging organizations for the disabled, schools and early intervention programs to have a "sibling day" or to sponsor a sibling workshop.

Parents can also establish informal sibling support groups through their own networks.

Having a child with a disability in the family is an opportunity for those living with that child to understand human differences in a way most people never get a chance to experience. Non-disabled siblings are in a position to teach others compassion and concern for those less fortunate. Furthermore, they have a chance to develop coping skills most children with siblings don't develop.

For that opportunity to be realized, however, these children need positive models and help from the adults in their lives if they are to learn to handle situations for which there are often no easy solutions. There will be many lapses between the "knowing" and the "doing," and the parent who understands this will be in a better position to help and will, ultimately, have competent and compassionate children.

PART III

Siblings

In the following articles, seven young men and women describe their relationships with sisters or brothers who are disabled. The issues they detail are similar to those discussed by the authors in Part II. Again, the issues raised are familiar to all sibling relationships, but are often particularly poignant in relation to the impact of the sister or brother with a disability.

In the first paragraph of "The Other Children," Victoria Hayden writes, "With love for my parents and for my deaf sister, I would like to speak for 'the other children' of exceptional parents." With empathy and sensitivity, Hayden praises and criticizes her "understanding parents" and, most of all, takes us inside herself as she grew up with her sister, Mindy, who is one year younger and deaf. With many vivid examples, she documents the positive and negative impact of growing up with Mindy.

Reminded to be nice to her sister, Hayden was angry and resented the different expectations and rewards she confronted and the extra help and attention her sister received. While Mindy's misbehavior was often accepted because she "could not help it," Hayden herself was chastised for such behavior. At the same time, while she felt she was expected to be an "exceptionally good little girl," no matter how good she was, her sister got more attention. Thus, she felt more was expected, less was given. Similarly, her sister's accomplishments were highly praised; hers were expected.

From early in her life, Hayden felt she had a "special responsibility" and was a "second mother." Often asked to be a baby sitter for her sister, Hayden describes the impact of her responsibilities on her social life with her peers as well as her role in her family. Her younger sister was a "drag" who contributed to her loneliness and feeling shunned. She also describes her concern about her sister getting lost while she was responsible—a theme discussed in another article.

Hayden tells about many fights and tantrums with feelings "openly expressed." Yet, in high school, with their father overseas in Vietnam, the Hayden sisters grew close and provided companionship and comfort for each other.

Julia Ellifritt reviews her life with her older sister, Bonnie Marie, who has Down syndrome. She vividly describes her struggles in a family setting in which, in contrast to Hayden, negative feelings were forbidden. She illustrates how these prohibitions made her more angry and led her to "abuse" her older sister. She wrote "Life with My Sister" to educate families about the importance of open communication.

Ellifritt wished for her own identity and wanted to be separate from her sister, but her mother dressed both girls alike and expected them to do things together. Like Hayden, Ellifritt feels that she became isolated as friends left her. She too shares a painful memory of when she thought her sister was lost.

Life changed for the better when the family moved to a new community and Ellifritt's church group's interest in her sister made it possible for her to get involved. As her peers accepted her and her sister, the relationship between the two sisters improved. Citing the value of her own personal therapy and participation in a support group for siblings, Ellifritt can look back and appreciate the influence Bonnie Marie has had.

Some of Eric Forbes' experiences with his older brother, who is hyperactive and has a learning disability, are similar to Ellifritt's with her older sister. In "My Brother Warren," he describes how it seemed that he and his brother had to do the same things, including giving up sweets and adhering to a special diet, and that his parents ignored his desires. He felt "left out and resentful" and believed that his life could have been normal were it not for his brother.

As a teenager, Forbes' social life contrasted with his brother's and he began to realize how difficult Warren's future life was likely to be. As he observed the nature of Warren's difficult relationships with his "friends," he gained more understanding. Looking back at the times he teased his older brother and made fun of him, Forbes expresses regret for his own behavior. While he believes he has had a difficult life because of Warren, Forbes feels these experiences have made him "a more patient person and caring person." He now knows he can live with his brother and loves him: "It just took me a while to realize it."

Perry Dubinsky felt cheated because his brother is mentally retarded. He kept wishing for a day when his brother "would wake up and be like me." Although we do not learn the details of the sibling relationship in "My Special Brother," Dubinsky does tell us that until he began to accept his brother and his disability, he turned his back on his brother's pleas for affection. As he accepted the situation, he became more understanding and was able to help his brother.

In "Away from Home for the First Time," Michael Levitt gives us a glimpse of his loving family, which includes his younger sister, Stacy, who has cerebral palsy. He shares his realizations about just what Stacy has taught him—especially "never to judge people without understanding them first."

Jennifer Dickman's brother, who has Down syndrome, is two years older than she. Her story, "Courage in Adversity," is positive from the beginning. She went with Dick to therapies as well as recreation events and grew up knowing people with disabilities as people. She and her brother were expected to follow the same rules and standards of behavior; she accepted his superior knowledge of baseball along with his intellectual limitations.

When Dick was diagnosed with leukemia, everyone in the family had a difficult time. Dickman describes her brother's courage through six years of treatment and feels she learned a great deal from him during this time.

"Dear Mom" also tells a positive story; yet, it is a different kind of article about sibling and family relationships because it illustrates how the understanding of a caring parent can contribute to a relationship of a brother and sister. The article is a letter Paul Pendler wrote to his mother the night before Lisa, his 23-year-old sister who has Down syndrome, moved to a group residence. His letter is a tribute to his mother in which he thanks her because she "permitted me to explore my own feelings of anger and guilt" and never "let me feel that I had to always be happy about having a disabled sister." His mother also let him know that Lisa "had her own special values, even though she looked different."

Although throughout the article he describes situations in which he "took advantage of her," Pendler conveys his understanding and love for his sister as well as his pride in her accomplishments. He shares how his mother, as a single parent, and their friends and neighbors helped and supported one another. He feels his life has been enriched and that he has learned sensitivity from his sister.

The Other Children

Victoria Hayden

All of the members of my family are disabled. But most people recognize only the disability of my deaf sister. They do not realize that the disability of one member affects the entire family. Parents realize this to some extent because they themselves are affected—their attitudes, their priorities, their life styles. But sometimes they become so involved with the problems directly related to their disabled child that they lose sight of the effect upon the other children. With love for my parents and for my deaf sister, I would like to speak for "the other children" of exceptional parents.

SPECIAL RESPONSIBILITY

I first remember having a sense of special responsibility for my deaf sister when I was three. It was my duty to keep her out of danger and mischief—a seemingly normal responsibility for an older sister. But the responsibility has at times felt unbearably heavy. As a two-year-old, Mindy was not only typically rambunctious, she lived in a bizarre and often dangerous world all her own—separated from the rest of us by her deafness and her inability to communicate. It was a world of fascinating objects to handle, of races with Mother, Daddy and big sister—a world, even, of nocturnal romps in the street while the rest of the family slept. And once, it was a world of pretty colored pills in the bathroom medicine cabinet.

Even at three, I knew something was wrong as I followed the trail of yellow toilet paper into the bathroom where Mindy was playing with the pills—gobbling up some and spitting others in the toilet. I woke my parents, and Mindy was rushed to the hospital where her stomach was successfully pumped. A later inspection of the house revealed that sometime during that evening Mindy had also mixed instant coffee in my brand new "Sunday" shoes. Although I vaguely remember feeling proud of "doing the right thing" when I discovered Mindy with the pills, I more clearly remember feeling hurt and angry about what Mindy had done to my new shoes.

I knew that my friends' younger brothers and sisters made messes and sometimes tore up books and toys, but nothing they did could compare with Mindy's constant destructiveness. If Mindy had been just plain bad I could have felt vindicated in the knowledge of her "badness." But Mindy was not "bad." She was deaf, and as yet without the skills of speech and lipreading. Part of me knew it was unfair to be angry with my deaf sister for filling my shoes with coffee. Still, in another part of me, the resentment lingered.

Did I express my feelings of dismay and hostility? Yes, thank goodness. Given the fortunate combination of understanding parents and my "can't keep quiet" nature, emotional outbursts were not suppressed.

Among the "other children," feelings of resentment, hurt and neglect can often manifest themselves in otherwise inexplicable developments: sudden troublemaking in "good" kids; learning difficulties in bright students; tall-tale telling and other attention-getting devices. As a teacher of the deaf, my mother knows many families with disabled children. And in many cases, at least for a time, the most difficult family problem has been with one of the non-disabled children—usually the oldest child upon whom the largest share of the caretaking responsibility falls.

"SECOND MOTHER" TO MINDY

When Daddy spent a year in Korea, I became Mother's sole helper. My role as second mother to Mindy held some prestige and much responsibility. It took away from play-time with children my own age. And, just as a mother serves as an example for her children, I was expected to be an exceptionally "good" little girl. The high standards my mother set for my behavior, though, had not only to do with my setting an example; her reasons were also practical. Mindy's impetuous behavior left her with little patience, energy or time to put up with shenanigans from me.

As I got older, problems resulting from my having a deaf sister increased. My mother began to attend college, and the new pressures and demands caused her to be demanding and dependent upon me. I did not understand why I would be severely chastised for the same behavior that Mindy, who embodied the behavior problems of three children, "couldn't help." My friends' parents seemed less critical of their children than my parents were of me. Mother and Daddy "expected more" from me, but it seemed to me that they gave me less.

The responsibility I felt for Mindy was tremendous. One year, when my "babysitting" duties involved periodic checking on my sister, Mindy wandered away between checks. After a thorough but fruitless search of the neighborhood, my mother hysterically told me that if anything happened to Mindy I would be to blame. I felt terrified and guilty. I was seven.

CONSTANT COMPANION

With the advent of school, I began to have more and more associations with other children. But wherever I went, Mindy went too. For I was her constant companion. Mindy's "differentness" rubbed off on me in the eyes of my playmates. I was the sister of "that deaf kid." Mindy was a "drag" for me and my playmates. She was difficult to communicate with, wild and stubborn. I was often excluded from neighborhood games because of my sidekick. And then there was the unwritten family rule that I must leave with Mindy whenever my playmates made fun of her. They often did mock her, of course, and we would leave—except for one time which to this day gives my conscience no rest, when I joined in. I lost many playmates by having to side with Mindy. I felt neglected by my family and shunned by my peers. I was a very lonely little girl.

COMPETITION AND RIVALRY

Mindy's eventual gift for language enabled her to enter public school after only five years of training in speech and lipreading. She was now completely a part of my world. She attended my school—just three grades below me. And a new competition crept into our relationship.

Mindy's achievements always met with animated enthusiasm from our parents. In contrast, it seemed, Mother and Daddy's response to my accomplishments was on the pat-on-the-back level. I was *expected* to perform well in every circumstance. I wanted my parents to be enthusiastic about my accomplishments too. I didn't want to have to beg for praise. I didn't want to be taken for granted. I wanted to be noticed.

Even though I realized it was necessary, I was resentful of the extra guidance Mindy received in school. I ignored her successes and scoffed at her failures. I especially resented the tendency of teachers to give Mindy "the benefit of the doubt." Such resentment sounds terribly unsympathetic. But Mindy has never conformed to the stereotype of the persistent, diligent, handicapped child. Despite her deafness, Mindy is academically very capable. But she doesn't like to work. She has all too often "conned" her teachers into pitying her rather than making her work.

As Mindy developed her language skills, she would interrupt, not having seen that lips were moving. Or her face would assume a puzzled expression, and she would ask, "What are you talking about?" All conversation would stop and all attention would be directed toward a special explanation for Mindy. It seemed to me that I was never able to complete a conversation with my family.

Because Mindy and I usually sat together in the back seat of the car while traveling, "Explain to your sister . . ." was an all too frequent command. I knew that Mindy's deafness affected her conversational fluency. And it was unfair of me to resent her interruptions and questions. My attitude was "It's not my fault Mindy is deaf." Sibling love is never easy. It is certainly not "automatic." Parents who are aware of the rivalry and resentment, in whatever form, have a departure point from which to move on to realistically encourage more positive and loving feelings and behavior.

BABY SITTER AND MESSENGER

My role as constant baby sitter continually posed social problems for me. When my parents enrolled us in recreational activities, they would often put me in Mindy's age group. I especially remember the swimming lessons. The teacher was uncomfortable around my deaf sister, and vented his discomfort in an antagonistic attitude toward me. Mindy thought going to the swimming pool was a game. She would merrily splash about, oblivious to the teacher's instructions and ignoring my explanations. "Can't you do anything about that sister of yours?" he would bark. And I dreaded the embarrassment on the way out, greeting my friends as they prepared for the class which followed "the baby class."

When I was not baby-sitting, there was my role of "fetch and carry"— sometimes literally. Mindy's deafness prevented my parents from calling to her so I was appointed official messenger. "Go tell Mindy to come to dinner." "Go tell Mindy to come inside." "Go tell Mindy to clean up her room." At first I probably gloried a bit in my "authority." But that soon grew stale. I was expected to stop whatever I was doing and bear some message to Mindy. And I discovered that like the royal messengers of old, bearers of orders or bad tidings are not cordially received. In retaliation against the inconvenience and the hostile receptions, I made a point of being as bossy in my deliveries as possible—which resulted in acute mutual aggravation.

"SHE CAN'T HELP IT"

Then there were the relatives. "Vicki, be nice to your sister. *She can't help it.*" I grew to hate those words. Try to explain to a young girl that her wildcat sister "can't help it" when she destroys her sister's toys, continually disobeys her parents, lies and cheats. It seemed that no matter how good I was, Mindy always got more attention. With pity and that illogical sense of guilt that families always seem to have about a disabled member, they raved about how "cute" Mindy was and reproached me for not being more tolerant of her.

Some deaf children are less inhibited than hearing children with their affection, and Mindy was no exception. As an adolescent I was embarrassed by Mindy's public displays of affection, especially in front of my peers. No self-respecting teenager publicly admits to loving a brother or sister, particularly not physically. Mindy's bear hugs are still a bit overpowering, but today I would not trade them for all the social cliques in the world.

Fights, tantrums—there were many. "I hate you" and "I wish you were dead" were shouted more than once. And we meant it at the time. The scenes were ugly, but the feelings were openly expressed, rather than suppressed only to surface in puzzling, unrecognizable "symptoms" such as behavioral and academic problems.

LOVE AND RESPECT

In my junior year in high school, Mindy and I began to grow close as sisters. Our increased maturity and the circumstance of our father's being away in Vietnam caused us to turn to one another for companionship and comfort. In the process, we began to discover one another as individuals. We took time to understand our mutual antagonisms and to forgive each other a little. Mindy now understands that as a child my responsibility for her was immense and often intolerable, and that she thoughtlessly made it more difficult for me. And she has forgiven me for the hurt my resentment caused her. Differences between us will always exist, but Mindy and I now understand and respect each other's needs without resentment.

The impact a disabled child has upon the other children in a family is tremendous—in both a positive and a negative sense. Parents must not expect sainthood from their "other children." Most likely many years will pass before their non-disabled children will fully understand why their sister or brother "couldn't help it," why they were expected to be model children, why attention from their parents was rationed and why their parents sometimes seemed unduly critical and impatient. Until the "other children" do understand, their reactions may be "thoughtless" or "unfair." Before love can replace misunderstanding and intolerance, resentment must be recognized and accepted as a legitimate and even inevitable part of the struggle of growing up together.

Life With My Sister: Guilty No More

Julia Ellifritt

My sister, Bonnie Marie, is two years older than myself and has Down syndrome. She has influenced my life more than anyone else has or probably ever will. She manifests the true gentleness and unconditional love that comes only from God. Sure, I wish she were normal (although sometimes I do not wish she were normal, and that thought scares me). But I think that my experiences with Bonnie have made me a more tolerant, understanding person—one who does not judge people by outward appearances but who can see beauty in every person. However, maybe I am afraid to think that she has not been a blessing on my life.

My biggest problem in dealing with Bonnie has been guilt. I had not been able to forgive myself for the things I had done. I know that God has forgiven me. In fact, He is probably tired of me asking for His forgiveness. Maybe I would have felt better if Bonnie could have fought back—she never said anything bad to me, she never hit me. What is worse, when I would do something to her, she would stand there crying and say, "I love you anyway." She was defenseless and I abused her. Now, years later, I cannot go to her and ask for her forgiveness—she would not know what I was talking about—so I have to live with my guilt.

I now know that there is sibling rivalry in every family—that bad feelings are not uncommon. But, as a child, I was told that those feelings were evil.

I was supposed to be a good Christian and love and accept my sister when inwardly I did not. I concluded that there was something wrong with me.

It has been only recently that I have been able to come to grips with a situation that I had struggled with for twenty-two years without accepting.

MY OWN IDENTITY

Part of my struggle in dealing with Bonnie was a need for my own identity, apart from her. When we were toddlers, Mom used to dress us alike. Maybe she was trying to make Bonnie look normal. From this early age, I was linked to a retarded person. Although I do not actually remember back that far, over the years whenever Bonnie tells people "we used to be twins,"—her way of explaining why we were dressed alike—I am reminded of this problem. I did not want to be associated with Bonnie.

My parents talk about my sixth birthday. I wanted a party without Bonnie. Bonnie loved parties and would be upset if she knew she was missing mine. So Dad took her to a movie while Mom had my party. I feel bad about that now. I know how much my actions hurt my parents but why should I still feel guilty about wanting my own identity; wanting a time when I was the special one without having a "freak" next to me?

It is interesting to me that I cannot remember any pleasant memories of Bonnie from my childhood. Whether that is intentional or not, I do not know. My earliest memory of her is when I was in the third grade and we used to "play house." I would always be the mother and make Bonnie the naughty child. During our play times I would spank her. Only I did not pretend, I really spanked her. Since I could not express my anger to my family, I expressed it to Bonnie, the source of my feelings, in a way that looked like play.

During my grade school years I thought of Bonnie as a witch. She had long stringy hair and she was skinny. She drooled and twisted her fingers and had other unpleasant habits. My friends would come over to play, take one look at her, and some would actually turn around and leave. I felt like everything I did, Bonnie had to do also. I could not get away from her. If I took piano lessons, she had to take piano lessons. When I was in Girl Scouts, she was in Girl Scouts (Mom started a troop for retarded girls). She wanted to be like me, and yet I wonder what kind of a role model I was. And finally, the last straw—she was mainstreamed into my junior high school.

ADOLESCENCE

I wanted so much to be accepted by my peers, and yet no one would play with me because of my shadow—my "social disease" that would not go away. The kids at school would tease, take advantage, and play tricks on her and the other "special kids" in the lunchroom.

I remember on the bus, no one wanted Bonnie to sit beside them. One girl walked with a limp. Every day I would ask her if Bonnie or I could sit with her and she would always turn away and tell me the seat was saved. Day after day, no one sat beside her. She sat alone and we stood. One day I got fed up. I picked her books up off the seat and threw them at her. Then I sat on her and made enough room for Bonnie beside me. It was an uncomfortable ride home, but I was tired of standing and I wanted to show people that they would not "catch mental retardation" sitting beside Bonnie. When the girl got off at her stop, I watched her limp down the street and I cried because I had been so cruel. She was handicapped. Of anyone on the bus, she should have been understanding. She really hurt me. I wondered why no one understood my problem.

My biggest responsibility that year was to make sure Bonnie got on the bus each day after school. It was a simple task and not a problem until one day I could not find her. I panicked. She was not on the bus so I ran to her classroom. But she was not there either. I looked in the other rooms and ran back to the bus, but the bus was gone. I was so upset. I cried and cried. I would have to call Mom and tell her I had lost Bonnie. Bonnie was gone and it was my fault. I tearfully got through to Mom on the phone, just as Bonnie was stepping off the bus in front of our house. My mother wanted to know where I was. Why had I missed the bus?

FAMILY

In my family, we were not allowed to discuss our feelings about Bonnie. After all, she was retarded and if we said anything negative, we might hurt her feelings. Well, what about my feelings? Who was concerned about how I felt? I hated my sister for ruining my life. She hurt me and I felt pain. I can remember one time having to sit next to her in the car and being so disgusted with her that I wanted to vomit, yet her feelings were at stake so I could say nothing. I remember being so angry at her, and then feeling so guilty. She was defenseless. She could not help the fact that she was retarded. How could I be mad at her? I lay awake at night praying that God would forgive me for having such thoughts about my sister. The range and intensity of emotions were much too much for me to handle.

My parents never sat me down and said, "There is the problem. This is what's wrong with her. Do you understand? Do you have any questions?" My attempts to communicate with my parents were all in vain. I remember several times trying to tell my Mom how I felt and she would say, "Your feelings are wrong and you'd better change them."

It was devastating to always be told that my feelings were wrong, and yet still not be able to get rid of them. Besides feeling guilty about having angry feelings, I began to think there was something definitely wrong with me.

Right about that time, our family moved half way across the United States. This was my chance to start over. I was starting high school in a new town where no one knew me. I swore to myself that I would not let Bonnie hurt me anymore. In my mind, Bonnie suddenly disappeared.

"So, you're new in town. Do you have any sisters?" "No," was always my reply. Bonnie was not going to be my problem; she was not my sister. When other students would ask me about my brothers and sisters, I would simply lie. It was easier to lie than to explain. My plan worked for a few months until one night when I was at a Youth Group meeting at the new church my family had been attending. The leader introduced me, said I was new, and then told everyone I had a retarded sister. There went my alibi.

To my surprise, however, this group was different. They thought it was neat that I had a retarded sister. I talked about Bonnie and they were interested. They wanted to meet her, and to do something with retarded kids. So we planned monthly parties for the retarded kids in our community. I spent many hours phoning parents, planning activities, and putting together parties that turned out to be successes.

As my high school years wore on, I did a lot of volunteering and working in the field of mental retardation. That work continued until I went away to college. I enjoyed my work, yet I knew something was wrong. Something I could not put my finger on. After two years away, I transferred schools and moved back home.

I began to realize that I had all the patience in the world with profoundly retarded men, but if Bonnie looked at me wrong, I got mad. I was genuine and loving towards people more severely retarded than Bonnie, but my love for her was not genuine. I loved to tease her, even though I knew it hurt her and made her mad. It made me feel good. I knew then that I was not behaving rationally. Twenty-one years of unexpressed anger had built up inside me, and it was starting to come out in unfortunate ways. I was desperate to tell this to someone and get it off my chest but I had no one.

Without telling my parents, I went to a psychologist. I cried and cried and talked nonstop for one hour, paid sixty dollars, and left. He did not say two words to me the whole time and I felt like he did not really understand me, but I got it out. On the way home, I started thinking to myself, "You just paid sixty dollars to someone who didn't say much. You could have told all that to a friend and it would have been cheaper." Then I said to myself, "No, Julia, you don't have a friend that you could tell it all to. In fact, the walls probably wouldn't listen." I cried again.

CHANGES

I should have been glad that I won the admiration of peers and adults, but I felt they were not seeing the whole picture. They would tell me, "You sure are a patient person. I admire the work you've done," or, "You've handled your situation well. I would never have been able to live with a retarded sister." Politely, I would thank them. Inside my heart would cry out, "I did not choose to be in this position. If *you* had a retarded sister, you would learn to handle it. And maybe I haven't really handled it at all, but I can't tell you that now. You wouldn't love and respect my anymore. Why can't you let me be human?"

I began to realize that I had been doing all kinds of work with the mentally retarded partly to assuage my negative feelings for my sister. I felt that in God's eyes I was making amends—that good works made up for bad thoughts. That was a scary thought. I did not want to think that all those years of work were done in vain. On the contrary, I enjoyed my experiences, and my life has been enriched by some very special people.

I was a college senior majoring in social work. I knew I would never be able to help anyone as a professional unless I could deal with my own feelings. I knew then that I could not do it alone. With the help of an excellent therapist, I began a healing process that was very painful, but very much overdue. I went to a support group for siblings of the retarded, and for the first time in my twenty-two years, I talked to others who had a retarded sibling. The relief and joy I felt was indescribable and will be forever etched upon my memory.

I am learning how to deal with my negative feelings and I am on my way to becoming a better communicator. I now realize that Bonnie possesses many of the qualities Jesus had—a gentle spirit, pure unconditional love, and selfless giving. I can learn from her. I am on my way to becoming more like her.

DEDICATION

This story is for Bonnie. With it, I pledge to do my best to educate other siblings as to the importance of feelings and family communication so that no other sibling need suffer silently. Bonnie may never read these words, but one day I know they will be inscribed in her heart and she will understand.

I have hopes that one day I will see her in heaven, and as we walk the streets we will embrace and cry, talk and giggle, and do the things that all sisters do; the things I have been deprived of in this lifetime. And we both will understand. Until then, I have my story. I can close the book on that part of my life, and I vow never to feel guilty about it again.

My Brother Warren

Eric Forbes

Sometimes I wish I could kill my brother, yet other times I wish I could love him. My brother Warren is twenty-one years old, hyperactive, severely learning disabled and still living at home with us. I am finally able to live in peace with him after seventeen years of constant fighting.

On Oct. 15, 1965, my brother Warren was born. My mother was in the delivery room for twenty-eight hours, and when he finally arrived, it was by the use of surgical prongs. By his second birthday, my parents knew there were long-term effects from the birth. He was constantly running around. They had to encage his bed because he was a violent sleeper and used to kick himself out. He was a consistent bed wetter until he was ten, which absolutely used to make me ill. He entered regular kindergarten but during the first grade was put into a special education class.

After I was born, he was jealous of all the attention I got, so he used to cry all the time. Anything that happened to me always had to happen to him and vice versa. When I had my fifth birthday, he had his, and if he didn't, he would run around and spoil my party. Afterward, he would invade my toy chest and break everything inside. Warren is a very heavy-handed person, and he breaks almost everything, even to this day.

SHARE AND SHARE ALIKE

By the time Warren was in second grade, he was diagnosed as hyperactive and started taking Ritalin. When he took Ritalin, I took vitamins because everything we did had to be the same. With his hyperactivity came very violent mood swings. He used to beat me up until I was bleeding before my parents could get him off me.

When I did anything wrong, he took it upon himself to discipline me by screaming or yelling, something he still does today. So every time I did something wrong, I was yelled at twice. He also cursed constantly. Every other word out of his mouth was a curse. When he was younger he used his cursing to get attention, but now that he has gotten used to it, he just can't stop.

NO MORE SUGAR

When my parents found out my brother had this problem, they at first decided to accept it and let life take its course. As things got progressively worse, they started to look for help. They went to a doctor who told my mother that all artificial preservatives and sugary foods would make Warren "fly." After I was seven we never had anything sweet in the house again. We made daily trips to the health food store and started eating lots of cheese and dairy products. We experimented with what he could and could not eat.

My parents totally ignored what I wanted and changed my whole life style. When you are seven years old this is very discouraging, like a slap in the face. I felt very left out and resentful. Because of him everyone was ignoring me. Because of him, no more sweet foods were allowed, no more potato chips or sugared cereals. We all adopted this new diet; I hated it and still do. I kept telling myself, if it wasn't for him then I'd be living a normal life. Now I see things differently.

BEGINNING TO UNDERSTAND

When I was eight years old we went on a trip to Puerto Rico, and my parents took us to the pool to swim. While they were sitting there, my brother got a little too rowdy and tried to drown me. I remember my parents waving, thinking we were playing and my brother laughing, like it was a big joke. The next thing I remember was waking up in the hotel room. He had almost killed me, and he didn't even understand what he had done. He said he was sorry and asked me to go swimming with him again. I then began to realize and understand his problems.

When I entered high school, he entered it too. He started normal classes in the eleventh grade. It became very hard for me. He could treat me like dirt at home, and I understood, but not in school.

Toward the middle of the year I became more understanding. I saw a group of his "friends" making fun of him and laughing at him. It was then that I started to understand what was making him so antagonistic.

He had become the manager of the lacrosse team, and every night when he came home after practice, he was so frustrated. He would scream at everyone from the paperboy to my mother, to my dad and me. After this happened a few times, I went to a practice to see what was making him act this way. The lacrosse players were animals. They would put him on top of a hill, push him down and say "roll Warren roll." As he rolled over and over again, they laughed and laughed. It was disgusting, but no matter how badly they treated him, he was so happy to be one of the guys that he put up with it. He was the manager for two years, and for those two years we all knew that, when he got home, we had to stay out of his way.

DEVELOPING SOCIAL LIFE

As school went on, my social life got better and better. I became rather popular, while my brother had no social life whatsoever and struggled to keep the friends he had. I started to see the problems he was going to have all through his life. Then one day I walked into Syms, a department store where he works, and he said to all the employees, "There's my brother. Isn't he cool?" I wanted to run up to him and give him a big hug and kiss, but I knew that was not his style.

He started to ask me questions about the girls I was dating and tried to get all the details about them out of me. He wanted to know where we went, what we did and anything else he could pry out of me. He was living my life because he had no social life of his own. Every time a girl broke up with me, he told me that he didn't like her anyway. If I broke up with a girl, he'd tell me that it was the right decision. At twenty-one, he has never had a girlfriend.

A NEW REALIZATION

I now look back at all those times when I made fun of him, teased him or even called him retarded and wished I didn't. He is a very caring brother. He used to give his clothes away to the poor when we vacationed in Jamaica. He would give me the shirt off his back. He's my brother, and I am now able to live with him and get along with him instead of wanting to keep him out of my life. I love him; it just took me a while to realize it. I have had a hard life living with him, but I think that it has made me a more patient and caring person. One day I will look back at all our experiences together and smile, because I was a part of helping him to grow up.

My Special Brother

Perry Dubinsky

The titles are endless: mental retardation, autism, Down syndrome, cerebral palsy. People. Sheltered from our world, they are shunned by society, all but forgotten by our communities. The world they know is theirs, and theirs alone. As people not afflicted with any mental or physical disability, we may push them aside, unwilling to accept them, yet willing to avoid the burden they present to us. Because they are harder to deal with, because they do strange things, things that are not "normal," we are unwilling to accept them as part of our society. Dealing with special children is difficult and, so, many people don't. If any one of those people that ignore the situation would gather the courage to spend even a short amount of time with a retarded child, they would immediately sense the many needs of the child.

As the sibling of a mentally retarded child, I felt cheated because my brother was not the same as other kids. I was waiting for the day he would wake up and be like me, a day that will never come. So many times he pleaded for the affection he desperately needed and so many times I turned my back and ignored his appeal. I did not understand.

Finally, I came to accept his condition, and from there I was able to help him. Acceptance leads to understanding, which in turn leads to helping, assisting.

Like all special children, my brother's love for everyone and everything around him is wholly genuine. He has no ulterior motives attached to his smiles and hugs. All of the kids, from the highest functioning independent child, to the lowest functioning who is dependent for all his or her needs, sense attention and respond to it. The value of the return outweighs the investment. When they respond, we do not see sadly deformed or mentally disabled people. We see regular human beings, happy to be alive.

We are the ones that shower pity on them while they enjoy life, regardless of their disability. They don't have the worries and complexities of normal life. Often we express our desire to become children again to escape, which is exactly how they live their lives. Seeing them perform and progress holds an indescribable gratification. Adjectives written on a page are inadequate to describe the lives of these wonderful beings. How, in a land booming with technology, can we turn our backs? We must further our involvement, in every fashion, and strive to make better the conditions in which they, and we, function.

Reflections of a College Freshman: Away from Home for the First Time

Michael Levitt

Returning home from college thrills me because I am privileged to be greeted by my sister, Stacy. "Michael home, Michael home," she cries as I walk in the door.

"Brother Mike here, play piano," she continues as I take off my coat.

"Fix record player, pleeease," she exhorts as I sit down for a luscious meatballs and spaghetti dinner prepared by our next-door neighbor.

Greetings like these make me realize just what Stacy has meant to me.

My sister Stacy is mentally and physically disabled as a result of cerebral palsy. She cannot walk very much, nor talk very much, but she has more intelligence than many "normal" people and is so easy to love that people who meet her once can hardly forget her warmth. Stacy can brighten up a room with a single smile and cheer up a friend by raising her eyebrows and giving a hug. I wish that I was as super a person as she is.

"Swallow," I tell Stacy to remind her to refrain from drooling. Stacy and I understand that "swallow" is more a term of mutual love than one of reprimand. So is "dry girl," my reminder to Stacy not to wet her bed. Whenever I utter either of these phrases to Stacy she usually obeys them, gives me a kiss, and then grabs my arm and pulls me to the piano where I play her favorite song, "I've Been Working on the Railroad." Somewhere Stacy picked up the femme fatale trick of exchanging kisses for favors. I told you she was intelligent.

Stacy has taught me to never judge people without understanding them first. A hasty judgment of Stacy does not reveal her acute perceptiveness. Only when she sneaks into my room while I am asleep and takes out my clothes for the following day (matching yet!), or brings me the *TV Guide* opened to her favorite show (Murder She Wrote), although she can in no way read, are her very human traits revealed. As a result, I hesitate to classify other people too quickly as one type or another until I have some better understanding of them. I always laugh when my Hopkins roommate suddenly turns to me and says, "That guy is gay," or, "Jack's a nerd," after seeing them but once. So many people judge books by their covers. Stacy taught me not to.

Stacy has also forced me to mature quicker than I otherwise might have. After our father passed away, I virtually became Stacy's father as well as her brother, her private chauffeur, her Chanukkah Santa Claus, her Mr. Fix-it, as well as her piano man. A fine line definitely exists between parenthood and slavery.

When I left for college Stacy apparently misunderstood and feared that I had left forever just like our father had. Sunday night phone calls and my visit home for Yom Kippur convinced Stacy that I was all right.

Relatives and friends say that Stacy is lucky to have a family like ours, but I think that actually my mother and I are lucky to have a very special child like Stacy.

"Swallow, Stacy." Or in other words, we love her.

Courage in Adversity: My Brother Dick

Jennifer Dickman

Once upon a time, a little boy, named Dick, was born with one too many chromosomes. Down syndrome is the clinical description. He was a cute, chubby baby who progressed slowly but steadily. Life was beautiful and simple for Dick and he embraced it with enthusiasm. Two years later a little girl, named Jennifer, was born with exactly the right number of chromosomes. A normal, healthy girl was her clinical description. This story is about the bond between the two and the positive effect his life has had upon hers.

As children, Dick and Jennifer were inseparable. Dick always referred to Jennifer as "My Jennifer." Jennifer accompanied Dick to his never-ending speech lessons, special schools and Special Olympic meets. For Jennifer, people with disabilities were just that—they were *people* first.

Slowly, Jennifer began to realize that she was able to do things quicker and better than Dick. She wondered if he realized too. Perhaps not, for this type of comparative thinking was difficult for Dick. At any rate, when Jennifer won the tug-of-war at her class picnic in fifth grade, Dick was there cheering. When she received the "Citizenship Award" from her elementary school, Dick told everyone he met. One day, during a car pool pick up, someone new asked Jennifer why her brother spoke so funny. "It's simple," she said. "Your sister has a broken arm. Well, Dick's brain is a little broken." Acceptance of Dick's condition was a fact of life for Jennifer.

Values and outlooks on life were being formed during these years. Jennifer learned to judge people on their own merits rather than on a person's disability. People's reaction to her brother became a gauge. Of course, there were a few children in school who stared and made fun of him. However, by and large, those who took the time to get past the "difference" became lasting friends.

The same rules and standards for behavior were applied to Dick and Jennifer. Once, when Dick, unannounced and unaccompanied, walked away—quite far away—to the park and was returned by the town police-man, Jennifer proclaimed to the neighborhood children that Dick was being punished and had to stay in the house all afternoon!!

Retardation is a harsh and difficult word, but Jennifer knew it was just a word and preferred to use Down syndrome when referring to Dick's condition. She knew quite a lot, at this point, about the causes of and prognosis for people developmentally delayed with this syndrome. She was comfortable with her life and simply accepted the fact of Dick's slowness, just as she accepted the fact of his superior baseball knowledge. Life for Jennifer and Dick was just fine.

Then, one cold, windy day in January everything crumbled. Dick was diagnosed as having acute lympholbastic leukemia. Could this be possible? Wasn't Down syndrome enough? As Dick left for the hospital the next day, he called a bright "good bye" to Jennifer, telling her that he would see her soon.

Treatment was horrendous for Dick. The chemotherapy wasted his body, the radiation burned his skin. The bone marrow and spinal tap tests without anesthesia were medical torture. There were weeks when Dick spoke to no one, save Jennifer. He anticipated their Sunday night visits, which seemed to refuel and recharge his determination to endure.

Initially, Jennifer was angry and greatly saddened. She functioned as if in a trance. She did her assignments, helped her grandmother at home with chores and watched over her baby brother and sister. All the time, her mind struggled with questions of "Why?" and "To what purpose?"

Slowly, as the shock of the illness settled, Jennifer became aware of Dick's great courage. Her visits to Dick were difficult but she knew how greatly he counted on them. He would block out the pain to talk to her. He would tell her of his recent tests that were so traumatic. He would say good-bye with the words, "Next Sunday."

In August, 1987, Jennifer helped get ready for the great celebration party which ended Dick's treatment, six years after it had begun. She looked at Dick opening gifts from friends, neighbors, and family, equally delighted with a pack of baseball cards as with the Sony Walkman. His cheeks were chubby again and his eyes sparkled with that old enthusiasm for life.

Jennifer thought about Dick's courage in adversity, his pure delight in life's pleasures and simple acceptance of events over which he had no control. These qualities are intrinsic to Dick and, through knowing him, have been learned by Jennifer.

The little boy who was born with the wrong number of chromosomes taught much to the little girl who was born with exactly the right number.

Dear Mom

Paul Pendler

I am giving these thoughts on living with a disabled sister to you as an early birthday present, and also because I know you would be happy to read what I wrote. I decided to write it tonight, while sitting at home after Lisa left for Chelsea Residence and after seeing how inwardly hard it was hitting you. It felt good to explore my vast feelings because, for me, not dealing with it has been dealing with it.

I know we did the right thing in letting Lisa live in an independent environment, but it sure does take some getting used to.

I have a sister who has Down's syndrome. Lisa is twenty-three years old. At twenty, I am her younger brother. Recently, for a number of reasons, I have thought more and more about life with her. First, Lisa has been preparing to move to a group residence for at least a year, but these last few weeks prior to her moving have been intense. Coupled with this, I have had more time at home because of the intersession of my university. The college break has allowed me to re-enter home life and see my sister as she is.

My family has undergone a series of crises. When I was one year old, my father died. My mother would not have a husband, and we would no longer have a father to share in our family's growth and development. Coping with such a problem is very hard. To this day, I am not sure how my mother did it, but in her amazing way she did. Perhaps it helped her to get out the feelings and try to deal with them as best she could.

We were lucky my mother had friends, good ones, who knew the meaning of helping someone in need. These friends babysat for me and Lisa so my mother could go out and be free of the turmoil in her life for a while. These friends accepted all of us and treated us with care and love, but never patronized us. They never made us feel like the "sad old Pendler family with all their problems." These friends helped all of us grow by giving of themselves in their small ways. To this day, they still offer the same care and consideration. Without our friends, I don't know where we would all be.

A SECOND FAMILY

Growing up, I was also blessed with neighbors. Mr. Duban was the superintendent of our building and his family became our second family. The Dubans met my parents when we moved into the apartment, and they lived here until I was fourteen years old. My mother is a New Yorker and thrives on going to the theater and having dinner with friends in the city. The responsibility of caring for two children, one of them mentally retarded, could have forced her to give up some of the things she enjoyed most, but the Dubans helped out. I know now she needed time by herself to help her be a better mother to us and help her cope with having a retarded daughter.

After school, we often stayed at the superintendent's apartment for dinner, and slept there until my mother came home. There I experienced the life of a large family, as well as my own special family life. From the Dubans I learned all the things that one tries to teach children as they grow up, how to go to the bathroom (standing up), as well as the meaning of giving and sharing. They accepted our family as part of theirs.

I had a father to talk to, to teach me and do things with me. I had an older brother who taught me about baseball and cars and sat around with me on the afternoons when my mother went out. I had a mother, in addition to my own, who gave me love, care, food, thoughtfulness and more than I am able to put into words. I had two sisters who taught me about growing up in that period, shared the joy of their holidays, and showed me how to give and not worry so much about receiving. They also had two dogs, a Guinea pig, and a parrot they named after me! They have moved to another town, and sometimes I feel a bit lost without them.

MY MOTHER HAS DONE SO MANY THINGS

It's my mother's college days I remember best, living downstairs at the super's apartment while she attended classes after work. My mother has managed to get bachelor's and master's degrees in community health education. Through my mother, I became associated with the anti-war movement of the sixties. I remember she took Lisa and me to the demonstrations while we were still in baby carriages. I met my mother's friends from all walks of life. They told me about their beliefs about life, war, living together, etc. I was shaped from all of these brief exposures, as well as by my sister.

There have been many things in my life that go unnoticed until the right moment comes along. My mother has done so many things. She is an inspirational person. Through Lisa, she became involved with the Association for Help of Retarded Children. She is quite active in this parents' group, and participates on many different committees. She helps other people who have retarded children, because in every sense she "has been there." Her efforts sometimes go unnoticed by her professional colleagues, yet she still maintains her drive. I am very proud to say that I have the same drive, although it has often caused problems for both of us.

I am in college now and studying child development. But I did not fully comprehend it until I thought about how I developed my own philosophies. I am lucky to have had these experiences with my mother, and even to have had all the arguments we had when I was younger. I was stubborn, as well as a little spoiled. Today, I would describe my arguments, or discussions, with my mother as an interaction between two people who are sometimes mother and son, sometimes two professionals, but always friends who care for one another.

MY MOTHER'S ADVICE

Probably, the most important advice I got from my mother was to openly deal with feelings. Never did my mother make me feel I owed something to her, that I had to be with her always because I had a sister who was retarded. She let me know very early on what Lisa was like, that she had her own special values even though she looked different. My mother permitted me to explore my own feelings of anger and guilt, as well as the joys of growing up. Too often parents of disabled people put a burden on siblings, expecting them to perform a parental role, not allowing them to develop and explore things by themselves.

My mother never let me feel that I had to always be happy about having a disabled sister, and in fact, encouraged anger about it, as long as I kept it in perspective.

At times I would ask my mother to have Lisa go over to a friend's house so that my own friends could come over, and she obliged. After a while, I stopped doing this and came to believe that my friends would have to accept Lisa the way she was. I lost a few friends this way, but they were not real friends, or they would have dealt with Lisa as a person.

I thank my mother for letting me feel as open about life with a disabled child as possible. I developed an interest in the field of special education, and I learned how to be with people who are different. But what I really learned is that they aren't so different. I now feel Lisa's friends are my friends too.

LISA IS REMARKABLE

Lisa is a remarkable human being. She is short and plump, not terribly attractive, but bursting with life and energy. She has limited reading and writing abilities but uses her social skills to compensate. She always seems to enjoy things no matter how routine. She can be happy sitting at home alone coloring and watching television or doing the rather tedious work she does at a sheltered workshop. When she was assigned to work in the cafeteria, her job entailed a lot of standing while putting away the clean plates. Lisa found a way, with a small bench, to sit down and relax while doing her job. Sitting down with a contented look on her face, she was putting her plates away, happy to have solved the standing problem.

I often wonder if Lisa is happy or if she understands life in general. She seems to make something out of anything and enjoy it. I think she has mastered the ability to take things in stride, no matter what. I am jealous because I don't always have that quality. Today she can do many different things, from cooking her own dinner to traveling the intricate system of confusion called the New York subway. To this day, I don't know how she manages to get a seat on the trains at rush hours. She attends a variety of activities on her own, including a dance club, swimming and social programs run by a variety of agencies.

As I look back now, I feel somewhat guilty that I haven't given enough of myself to her, but according to Lisa's friends and counselors she talks about me and seems to think I am wonderful. Perhaps I found a way to forget her by not doing so much with her. In spite of that, she thrives on the anger, excitement and satisfaction that I apparently give her. Every night, for instance, when she goes off to bed, she says "good night." My mother always manages to say "good night" back, no matter what she is doing, but I often grunt something that sounds like "goodnight." Lisa sounds gleeful at my responses, muttering in a soft voice, "Thanks!"

Maybe now that she will be living on her own away from us, she will remember whatever feeling I gave to her. Too often I know I took advantage of her, and now that she is away and I look at her empty bed, I wish I could have done more.

There were times when I would want to watch TV, and then go quickly into my room to listen to the stereo. I would just tell her to go out of the room, and she would oblige. Then in a matter of minutes I would want to go back to the living room. I would tell her to go back into the bedroom, and still she would oblige (I must admit that as she got older, she began to comment to herself how crazy I was).

I WILL MISS HER

Now that she will be living in the group residence, I do plan to visit and do more things with her, perhaps to justify her great admiration for me. It is sad I never noticed how much I took her for granted until Lisa was gone. Of course I am happy for some things; I now have a room to myself. We always shared a bedroom because we could never afford to move to a larger apartment.

I won't get frustrated as much at her shortcomings nor will I get angry when people stare. I will, however, be losing something. I will not be able to sit down and play our teasing little games of spatting with each other, and I will miss having someone, who, regardless of her understanding, can be here to do things with. I will not be able to share all her excitement now that she is gone, nor be able to feel her love for me.

I know my mother gets upset when she sees other people Lisa's age going off to college or out with boy friends, but having a retarded sister doesn't hit me in the same way. I don't look at her in terms of being mentally retarded; she is my sister, and that's what it is. I missed having an older sister to share feelings with, but I compensate through my friends. Perhaps I have accepted Lisa in spite of her handicap more than I realize.

Although Lisa's move into a group residence takes a great deal of adjustment, we have been living independent lives for some time. Lisa has been going off to the workshop and all her varied programs; I go off to school and out with my friends; my mother goes off to work and her activities. The time we spend together has decreased to the point, that, for the past few months, Lisa has already been on her own. However, lately, the little things like having breakfast or lunch together on a weekend became very special to me. I would talk to Lisa about her job. When I asked her how much money she made, she hesitated for a few minutes. She knew it made me more anxious to hear her answer and that I would be proud of her (she is not so dumb as that). These memories are moments to treasure.

I hope I always remain as close to Lisa as I feel at this moment. I doubt I will forget about her when I move into my own life; having lived with her has been such an integral part of my growing up. I also hope that she enjoys living in her apartment setting and remains as happy about life as she is now. Most of all, I wish more people could get the chance to meet her—talk with her, laugh with her, and just be with her, so that they, too, could experience the feelings I have had as her brother. I wish they could see how she lives in our society, and help to change the backward, somewhat barbaric views of others about mentally retarded people. I don't know if Lisa realizes how much she enriches the lives of those she comes in contact with, nor do I know if the people who come in contact with her realize her contribution.

I have experienced a special kind of life having a disabled sister, and in many ways, a more enriched life. I hope that once I start working with retarded people and their families, I can help them to understand the importance of being open with their feelings. I also hope I can use my career to open group residences that will allow all the qualities Lisa has to flourish and flow to others like herself. She is very wonderful in her own special way—just as we all are—in our own special ways. . . .

PART IV

Case Studies

The five articles that follow are clinical case studies of families in which a family crisis is sparked, in part, by the relationships between siblings, including one with a disability. Each case study is from "Family Life," a regular feature in *Exceptional Parent*, in which Maxwell J. Schleifer, Ph.D., a clinical psychologist and co-founder of the magazine, discusses a family seeking counseling and describes how, via the counseling process, the life of each family member is affected. The cases are from private consultation files; the names and circumstances have been changed to preserve confidentiality.

Each case study illustrates the complexity of human interactions and how parents' own childhood relationships with their parents later come into play as they raise their children. These case studies also demonstrate the continuing themes of sibling relationships: fairness, responsibilities, expectations, and the need for information.

In each of the families, we see the validity of the statement by Schreiber in his article "Forgotten Children" in Part I: "Sometimes parents feel that their child who is not disabled may need professional help . . . because they may react to special stresses in the family in unfamiliar or unacceptable ways." In addition, as the family crises in each of the families become resolved with the guidance and support of the psychotherapist, we appreciate Schreiber's further comments about how the unfamiliar or unacceptable behavior of the sibling without a disability can precipitate a crisis: "Such behavior may indeed be healthy and eventually constructive in that the child is not pushing his worries and questions down under, but letting them surface so that they can be faced and dealt with."

"I Get Upset When I See the Kids Playing with Jimmy" is the story of a family with three young children. Jimmy, the youngest, is not yet two years old and has severe physical disabilities. His parents, Mr. and Mrs. Costa, seek counseling because of their arguments about how much their daughters, ages four and six, should be expected to help with Jimmy's care. Although as a child Mrs. Costa had been expected to help her family, Mr. Costa believes it is wrong to ask their daughters to have any responsibility for Jimmy. With discussion, both parents realize that children need opportunities to help in family life.

In "When I Grow Up, I'm Never Coming Back!", fifteen-year-old Pamela Lebo feels she has been sacrificed because she is expected to care for her eight-year-old brother, Eliot, who has Down syndrome, much more than her older or younger brother. Her mother expects her daughter to be like she was when she was growing up and assume more responsibilities than her brothers. Part of Pamela's distress, now that she is a teenager, relates to her concerns about the genetic basis of Down syndrome. She is also a participant in a sibling discussion group, which has helped her confront her parents about her concerns.

In "Jerry Got Lost in the Shuffle," Mr. and Mrs. Quinn realize they have been expecting too much of their younger son, Jerry, who is now having difficulty in high school. Having advocated a great deal on behalf of their older son who has cerebral palsy, Mr. and Mrs. Quinn want to challenge the school officials to help Jerry. The parents describe how, in some ways, they have two different families, one with each child, and that Jerry may not have gotten the attention he needed.

As a college student, Donna Greeley has met other young adults who have siblings with disabilities. In her family, as described in "We Go Our Separate Way, Together but Alone," Donna has never been involved in the care of Julie, her younger sister who now lives in a residential treatment center. Her parents seemed to want to "protect" Donna from the "burdens" and did not discuss Julie with her. They even visited Julie without her. Donna used to feel ashamed about Julie and felt that no one needed to know that Julie existed. Now, Donna wants a relationship with her sister and urges her parents to bring Julie home for the summer.

As parents look to the future and try to plan to meet the needs of a child who is unlikely to be able to care for himself, they understandably turn to siblings. In "I'm Not Going to Be John's Baby Sitter Forever," a family crisis developed when Mr. and Mrs. Holmes met with their son and daughter, both young adults, to discuss their will in relation to the youngest sibling, John, who is developmentally disabled. Mr. and Mrs. Holmes were shocked by the reactions of their older children. As parents, they had always tried to consider the needs of each of their children and had appreciated how their oldest son, Jimmy, had willingly participated in John's care. In the course of counseling, the parents realized how in doing so much for all their children, they may have forgotten to address their own personal, adult needs.

I Get Upset When I See the Kids Playing with Jimmy

Maxwell J. Schleifer

"We're fighting all the time and I don't know how to stop." Mary Costa, a short, slender, blonde-haired woman in her early 30s, cried softly as she spoke. "Last week we got a note from the nursery school teacher that our four-year-old daughter, Julie, seemed very worried at school. Jim shouted that this was the last straw. We have a year and a half-old son, Jimmy, who was born with severe physical disabilities. Ordinarily, I have my six-year-old daughter, Jane, and Julie help with minor chores while I get dinner ready.

"I had just asked Julie to go over and play with the baby, and Jim told her to stop. We have been having arguments about how much our daughters should help with Jimmy. Ordinarily, I don't do anything when Jim tells our children what to do even if I disagree, until they go to bed. And then we air our disagreements and arguments begin. It keeps taking longer and longer for me to get over these painful discussions.

"Sometimes we hardly talk for days after one of these encounters. But yesterday I just broke down and started to cry in front of the children. Jim proceeded to take the two girls out to a fast food place for dinner, and I stayed home with Jimmy.

"I think Jimmy should be included as a member of the family just as our daughters were when they were babies. He didn't complain when Jane helped me with Julie. We've gotten into an awful trap that I think neither one of us can get out of by ourselves. We try to have some discussion after an argument and we swear that we are not going to fight again. But within a week, we go back and do the same thing. The major disagreement we have is about what the girls should do for Jimmy.

"My husband feels that the children should be spared. He says that Jimmy is our problem and that although we may have to pay a price, we should not rob the children of their own pleasure and fun in growing up. They'll have plenty of time to take on burdens when they are adults.

"I disagree. First of all, I'm the one at home. There is an awful lot to do. The kinds of things I ask them to do are appropriate for most four and six year olds—especially if they had a baby brother. I cannot do everything, particularly around dinner time. Asking them to set the table or try to amuse Jimmy is not inappropriate. He is delighted with their company and very happy when they are available.

"Maybe there are times when I want my daughters to do something with Jimmy and as a result they cannot go out and play with their friends. My husband and I differ in the way we were brought up. When I was growing up, I was expected to help. Both my parents worked. I was the oldest of six children, so life could not go on if I did not help around the house.

"Most of the time I enjoyed it. Sure, there were times when I was a teenager that I felt I was being taken advantage of. Sometimes, I couldn't go out with my friends to parties because I had the responsibility to take care of my brothers and sisters. They in turn took on responsibility when they were able. Everyone was expected to help as soon as they could put away their toys. But overall, we grew up liking each other even with our family arguments. And today I know that I can count on them.

"Here we have another difference of opinion. After Jimmy was born, my husband was reluctant to ask our families to do very much for us. I was so numb for the first few months; I really don't remember what went on. For that period of time, I found it hard enough to do things by myself; involving other people was just more than I could manage.

"My oldest sister offered to take the girls on the weekends. On occasion we let them go visit her, but this seemed to bother Jim a good bit. He felt that my family was intruding, that they commented on the way we were doing things, and almost everything they did for us he saw as a criticism.

"Finally, it became easier for me to keep them home than to let them visit. At the same time, Jim has a sister who lives near us and I have never heard from her. In his family, she was the oldest and she was never expected to do anything for anybody but herself. That's the way they are. In fact, my family cannot understand why we have not been more involved with Jim's family. I think his mother and father greatly disapprove of the way that I have asked Julie and Jane to help out.

"Sometimes I think that we will never be able to get along again. I wonder whether we will ever have any fun together again. When I really get down I think back to before Jimmy was born and what a wonderful time we had. I remember how much I enjoyed being with my husband and how much fun we all had together with the children. Sometimes I dream that Jimmy hasn't been born and we're back together again. To be honest, the dream of life without Jimmy sometimes gets me through the day. And then when I think that's what's done it, I feel ashamed of myself."

"What Mary doesn't understand is how confused I am by this whole thing." Jim Costa spoke quickly. "Mary is terrific. She has been a saint. She has done more things for all of us than any wife could ever have done for any family. I admire the amount of time and energy that she devotes to various medical programs to make sure Jimmy has the best chance growing up.

"She spends two mornings a week in a hospital doing physical exercises with Jimmy and then one morning a week the therapist comes to our house to do the exercises. We're also supposed to do some of the things ourselves. I work awfully hard. I get up early in the morning; I work all day; I come home. I try to get home before 7 p.m., so I can at least see the kids. Then we argue about whether I help out enough.

"I feel I do a lot more than Mary gives me credit for. I do a lot of the shopping. I pick up the things that she leaves lists for. Mary's so tired by 9 that she's often asleep while I'm still up doing things. I don't think I get credit for any of that. I'm also working overtime to pay our bills.

"But it is true that I get upset when I see the kids playing with Jimmy. It's all right if they do it by themselves, but I feel it is wrong to ask them to take over these responsibilities. We try to discuss how much Julie and Jane should get involved with the exercise program. One time when I met with the therapist who comes to our house, she made it clear that she thought everybody should be involved. She thought it would be wonderful if we could include the grandparents. It seemed that she wanted to make it a circus.

"Look, growing up was no picnic for me. My sister and my mother argued with each other as long as I could remember. She resented anything I asked her to do so I stopped asking. My parents didn't get along with their parents or my uncles and aunts. I grew up as if I were an only child—without anyone but myself.

"When we first got married, I loved her family. They were so open and generous. I don't know what has gotten into me that I seem to resent them so much. They make me feel like I'm a lousy father.

"Talking to my family makes me feel worse. I can't bring myself to ask them for anything. And I can't bring myself to tell Mary how critical they are of the way we are bringing up our children and what we do with Jimmy. I also think it is very helpful for kids to grow up and take care of their own business, and not necessarily get involved with the matters of other members of the family.

"I really want Julie and Jane to have a good time growing up. There has been an awful lot of sadness. I just don't want to see them as sad as Mary and I are sometimes. We are stuck, and I am not sure where we can make a beginning, but I know we can."

DISCUSSION

The Costas came because of their disagreement about the role their young daughters should play in the life of their son Jimmy, who was born with severe physical disabilities. Mr. and Mrs. Costa had disagreed about the extent to which Mrs. Costa involved her daughters in his play as well as care. Mrs. Costa's belief was that their son, Jimmy, should be included as a member of the family, as any other baby would be. They had no difficulty when their youngest daughter was born having their oldest daughter Jane play with her and help mommy feed her. The problem between them had increased during the previous month. The last straw for Mr. Costa was when they got a note from the nursery school teacher, indicating her concern about how upset Julie seemed to be at school.

Mr. Costa considered the note evidence that proved his case—that too much was expected of the young girls and that it was time to change. Mrs. Costa focused more on their relationship as the central issue.

Mrs. Costa had been surprised at how irritated her husband had been toward her in all areas of their married life, not just in relation to their daughters. Mr. Costa admitted that he found himself shouting or being angry in ways that he had never expected of himself. They both were particularly surprised by their current unhappiness because they both had thought that their married life had been very good.

Husbands and wives have images of the kinds of parents they are going to become even before the first child is born, as well as how they will live together as a family. Parents comes to a marriage with their own set of family experiences that shape these images. During the marriage, these images become modified by the realities of the actual relationship between the husband and wife, and the actual behavior of their children.

Mrs. Costa had grown up in a family in which all the children spent much of their time together, playing with each other and working with their mother around the house. She came from a large, extended family group, who spent much of their spare time and vacation time together. She expected that her own family would behave in a very similar way and had high expectations that she would continue a lifelong association with her siblings and her parents. She had admired her husband when she first met him because of his own independence. She found that he was able to make decisions without being overly encumbered by the attitudes of other people. This, she felt, was a weakness in herself, and an admirable quality in her husband, Jim.

Mr. Costa grew up with a sister who was considerably older. In his family, there was little expectation, because of the sex differences and the age differences, that they would do very much together. In fact, Mr. Costa felt more like an only child as he grew up. This was magnified by the fact that his family did not live near any relatives and spent much of their time doing their own work. Just as his wife had been attracted by his ability to make decisions without considering everyone around him, he was attracted by Mrs. Costa's large, warm, interrelated family. He saw himself as the father who would take care of the needs of his wife and his children as well as being an active participant in Mrs. Costa's family. They both were happy during the early years of their marriage and were heavily involved together and with Mrs. Costa's family.

Life dramatically changed with the birth of their son, Jimmy. Nothing in either of their experiences had prepared them for the anguish, the disappointment and the concerns that they had.

During stressful times, families have a style of working together. Mrs. Costa expected to turn to her own family for support and had received a lot of help from her mother during the first year of her son's life and some support from her siblings. Part of the disagreement with her husband began with his feelings that her family was now intrusive. He was not sure that he wanted them to spend so much time in the care and nurture of his own children and to make so many decisions about raising them.

At the same time, he found himself less available. Because of the large medical bills and incidentals that were not covered by their insurance, he found himself working a greater number of hours. At the same time, he had little support from his own parents or sister. When he called them, he found that they were critical of the kind of advice he and his wife had been getting from specialists.

Both Mr. and Mrs. Costa found themselves behaving in ways that they were unhappy with. They began to criticize each other at times when they both knew that they shouldn't.

Parents whose children are born with disabilities are unprepared for the amount of time and energy this stressful period will take. In the first phase after the birth, their energy is taken up as they try to absorb the meaning of the event and sort out what role it will play in their lives. Time and energy are spent reviewing and re-reviewing the experience to make some sense out of what has happened. This was a period of time that the Costas both describe as feeling numb.

During this time, people are most vulnerable to their own inner most concerns and fears. They both recalled how helpless they felt and wondered whether they were ever going to be able to summon the time, the energy and the courage to continue.

At a time when parents need to work together, the stress that they experience usually complicates their ability to communicate their own needs clearly. Unable to turn to one another, parents often struggle with their own needs for care and support. They often see themselves or the other partner as being selfish and are not sure how to change this behavior, either in themselves or in their spouses. The Costas knew they were doing things that they did not want to do but did not know how to stop. The more they argued, the more they stewed and each felt rejected and misunderstood.

People generally underestimate the time and energy that is required for parenting. This is considerably underestimated for the care of a child who has complications in growing up. All parents need to find ways of taking care of each other's needs as well as finding times to replenish their own emotional supplies if they want to meet the demands of continuously understanding and meeting the needs of their children. Parents do this by finding various ways of continuing aspects of their own social life, such as going out evenings or taking small vacations. The presence of a child with a severe disability who requires special attention can seriously impede the ability of parents to support one another and to supply the nurture and the respite that both need.

The Costas quickly related to their own need to spend time together alone. Each had thought about it independently; but whenever it was broached, it took place within the context of struggles about how to care for their son, Jimmy. The solution that was most readily available was to use members of Mrs. Costa's family to care for Jimmy while they found time for themselves. It also became clear to them that they had to do this not only so they could be better parents, but to preserve their marriage.

Parents commonly try to protect children from difficult experiences. They often believe that if they do not discuss their concerns, the children will not know about them. In fact, children are aware of when their parents are troubled. When they do not know why, their own concerns can be exaggerated. They can also believe they are at fault.

When children can help with a family problem, they often feel much better. Children with siblings who have serious disabilities generally have done better in their own lives if they were involved in helping. Both the Costas believed this. Both also recognized that too much involvement was not good. They had to discuss these issues and include their daughters whenever possible.

Mr. and Mrs. Costa met with me monthly during the course of the year. During this time, they were able to go back and look at their early relationship in the marriage. Mr. Costa was able to share with his wife how helpless he felt about providing for his son, and how when her family came in, it just made him feel even less capable as a father. As he began to understand the source of his own concerns, he was able to develop a better relationship not only with his wife, but with his in-laws. Mrs. Costa, at the same time, understood how important it was to discuss with her husband in advance the things that they might do for one another before she asked her children or family for help.

Mr. Costa recognized that Jimmy was a member of the family and his daughters had to be included with him. As he understood how his inability to do his ordinary fathering made him feel helpless, he realized that interfering with his daughters and their ordinary efforts to be good big sisters would be disruptive to them. Mr. and Mrs. Costa found that as they were able to work together better themselves, their younger daughter improved quickly at school and the general mood of the family improved. They also found that finding time to do things for each other and by themselves brought back the happy memories of the past.

When I Grow Up, I'm Never Coming Back!

Maxwell J. Schleifer

"My husband and I have been involved in battles with our fifteen-year-old daughter, Pamela, since she started high school last fall," Peg Lebo, a short, dark-haired woman in her mid-forties spoke quickly. "The battles are about many things. But last week things erupted when she was asked to stay home to 'baby-sit' our eight-year-old son, Eliot, who has Down syndrome.

"Pam began to scream that she has been sacrificed to care for Eliot. She claims our seventeen-year-old son, George, and her eleven-year-old brother, Michael, were never asked to spend as much time with Eliot, nor were they asked to do as many things as she does. She stormed out and said, 'When I grow up and am living on my own, I'm never coming back here again.' She said she never wanted to have anything to do with Eliot for the rest of her life.

"I know that sometimes kids feel this way when they are young. They say things to their parents, like never wanting to see them again—but they really don't mean it. I can remember saying something like that to my mother. Just the same, my husband, John, and I were both very upset by this outburst. For the first time, we began a lengthy discussion about the things that have been going on for the last eight years—since Eliot was born. We have tried to do this many times, but after ten or fifteen minutes we would stop talking. Each time we tried to reassure each other that everything was O.K. and that things would work out. This time we both were determined to see it through to the end.

"We started remembering when Eliot was born. All I could remember was what seemed like a state of shock that lasted for about a year. When John and I began to discuss our feelings about the experience, I was confused. Sometimes it seemed like I was numb until I got out of the hospital. Maybe the pressures began to ease when Eliot was about three. Our memories about critical events in Eliot's life are about the same.

"When Eliot was about six months old, we started taking him to a program at our local medical center. I met professionals and parents at the hospital who believed that something positive could be done for Eliot. That was the first time anyone had suggested we could feel hopeful about Eliot. They gave us practical advice about what we could do for Eliot and what we could expect from him. When he was about three, they felt we could move on to other pre-school programs, and I felt much better. We are still involved with that center. Each year Eliot has an annual check-up there.

"John remembered things a little differently. John says that we were told about some of these things before going to the center. He says other professionals had told us how much Eliot was capable of learning, but that I would not listen. John claims he could accept Eliot's disabilities long before I was able to. That is when we began to look into our personal wrangle.

"Sometimes it feels that we are separate islands in the sea. The islands sometimes talk to one another and sometimes they don't. I am the one at home with the daily responsibilities of taking care of all the kids. John takes care of the finances.

"Pam brought up something important. As the oldest daughter, she was expected to take over and help me with the family. She argues that she does the most and gets the least attention. When she spoke up, I began to realize that I have been feeling just the way Pam feels for the past eight years. I am the one that generally takes Eliot to the clinic, gets him off to school, attends the meetings, and goes to the doctors and therapists. My husband is involved in his work and his own pleasures. I don't want it to sound like John is a bad husband, but during our discussion I began to wonder about the kind of relationship we have.

"When Pam began to shout, John did something that ticks me off. He sided with Pam without hearing the whole story. Whenever we get in this sort of wrangle with our children, John always sides with the kids. He never sides with me and it always makes me look like the bad guy. I am the one that has to lay down the laws and he is always the one who can be so understanding.

"We had an agreement about the kids helping out by baby-sitting. In general, it is very difficult to get sitters. We don't have a lot of money and we have had to give up a lot of things because we didn't have a baby sitter. So I didn't see anything terrible about asking Pam to stay home.

"At first when Pam was shouting at us and saying that she did not want to have anything to do with me, I was shocked. I never had a very good relationship with my own mother, but I thought Pam and I had a good relationship. I only asked her to help with Eliot and her younger brother, Michael. I had to do the same kinds of things for my brothers and sisters when I was growing up.

"After the initial shock, I calmed down. Pam and I have done lots of things together. Last week was like waking up and finding out that our good family life was a dream—that in reality, it had not been very good.

"It wasn't just Pam's outburst that brings us here. John and I had our first long conversation in years. We reached a point in the conversation that was like a dead end. We didn't know where to go; we may have been too scared to continue; or maybe I was too frightened. I don't think that anything is going to be settled until we talk about the things that we have not dared to mention for almost eight years. I know we need some help."

"I think Peg is making more of this than she should," John Lebo, a stocky, dark-haired man in his late forties, spoke softly. "Peg makes it sound like, and she must believe, we have never talked at all. We do have a good relationship. We have been able to talk about all of Eliot's difficulties. But, the problems keep changing.

"Pam accused me of hiding and being selfish. I never thought of myself that way and her accusation was very upsetting. Granted, in the past couple of years, I have been doing a lot of things after work, like bowling and playing golf with my friends, but doesn't everyone? Our neighbors sure do.

"We have done a lot of things as a family. We have taken our kids on every vacation and camping trip. People have remarked that we have taken them places that they would not have attempted with their kids.

"I think Pam was very unfair. The boys have done their share. They have done all the heavy work around the house. As soon as George was old enough, he got a part-time job to take care of his own expenses. I also have a second job to help pay some of the extra costs in taking care of Eliot. That's another reason why I'm not home all of the time.

"I think Peg and I just have different ways of doing things. I don't disagree with Peg; I think Pam should help out. I just don't think there is time to get involved in lengthy discussions when someone is shouting. Peg reprimands the kids too much. When I come home, I need some peace and quiet.

"Peg feels she has the right to get into lengthy discussions no matter what else is happening. She is not willing to let something go. If she wants to discuss something, she will talk and talk and discuss it and discuss it. Then she feels it has been taken care of, that we both understand what we want to do, and we don't need to talk about it anymore.

"Pam just started high school and she has discovered a whole new world. She spends hours on the phone with her girlfriends talking about boys. I think that the 'dating age' would have been difficult, no matter what.

"Peg had fights with her own mother about dating. She was twenty when we first started to date. Her mother wanted to know where she was going, who she was going with and when she would be home. When she got home, her mother would ask her what she had been doing and why.

"I can remember my mother having fights with my sisters about the same kind of stuff. I was allowed more freedom because I was a son. Some of our problems are caused by the kids growing up. They are learning how to manipulate Peg. Sometimes I think we are allowing it to happen. Our kids, particularly Pam and Eliot, know all the right buttons to push. I think Peg and I should have had a discussion about their behavior a long time ago.

"We have never had a lengthy talk about what happened to our plans for a big family. If Eliot had not been born with a disability, we probably would have had another child. I think we both know that we do not want to have any more children, even though we have not discussed it. We have had much less sexual involvement than we might have because of the situation. I think we both have our own ways of dealing with it. When I wanted to discuss that issue the other night, the conversation ended.

"Lately, Pam has been asking her mother about being a mother and having children. Occasionally, she talks to be about her worries. She is trying to understand what causes Down syndrome; she wants to know why Eliot was born with it; and, she wants to know more about the hereditary issues. She has been going to a siblings group once a month. I don't know what to tell Pam or Peg. We seem to be stuck!"

DISCUSSION

Mr. and Mrs. Lebo sought advice after an argument they had with their fifteen-year-old daughter. Pamela claimed that her parents were taking unfair advantage of her by expecting her to take more responsibility for her brother Eliot. She also argued that she had new challenges and opportunities attending high school and that she was not being given a fair chance to pursue them. This argument was the culmination of a series of difficult discussions between Mrs. Lebo and her daughter since the high school year had begun.

The Lebos admitted that they did not know how to respond to Pam and her requests. They realized they had never fully discussed the nature of the requests they made on any of their children. They had so much to do helping their son Eliot that they had arbitrarily assigned household tasks and responsibilities without talking about them. Although there had been occasional complaints in the past, the children had been very helpful and seemed to appreciate the challenges that the family was undergoing. Mr. and Mrs. Lebo also recognized that they had never been able to sit down with one another to review their own lives and expectations since Eliot had been born.

The entry of youngsters into adolescence often changes the pattern of a family's interrelationship. Independent of the family, youngsters are starting on a path that will lead them to a sense of who they are and who they will become. Pamela Lebo was examining her family responsibilities, such as the time she spent "baby-sitting" her brother. She wanted time to take advantage of the new opportunities available in the high school—new friends, interests and activities.

With the onset of puberty, the adolescent also confronts parents with the issues of sex, drugs, cars, etc. Parents have to evaluate how to manage their child's demands for freedom and independence. Pamela wanted more time for her own activities but she shared her mother's anxieties about some of the activities of the high school youngsters.

The stress of helping a child with a serious disability grow has been fully documented. Families often cope by assigning family members responsibilities without considering alternatives. Later, families may continue to follow these patterns that were comfortable and successful in the past, even when they are no longer effective. After Eliot was born, Mrs. Lebo took over increasing responsibilities for all child-rearing. Mr. Lebo took on an extra job in order to meet the added expenses brought on by Eliot's disabilities. Pamela, the only daughter, joined her mother in helping to meet Eliot's needs. George, the oldest son, took over the "heavy work," such as yard work and small repairs around the house. George also found a part-time job to pay for his own recreational expenses.

A crisis can play a positive role in a family by forcing everyone to review their assumptions about the way they work together. When the problems have been identified, families may find it easier to change old attitudes and develop more appropriate ways to meet the present needs of everyone in the family.

The Lebos also reviewed questions they had about the birth of their son Eliot and the impact this had on their own sexual activity. Mr. and Mrs. Lebo recognized that they had to evaluate their own relationship. They had to bring their children in to review their responsibilities to the household.

There was a series of meetings in which every family member was included. The Lebos were surprised at their children's awareness of the way the family operated. Although the family was not eager to change, they were all aware of the problems that the existing situation presented. During the meetings, the family also listened to Eliot express his ideas about his activities. He indicated that he wanted to spend more time playing with his brothers and joining in their games, and he wanted to be able to join groups.

After four meetings, the Lebos decided that they would meet as a family once a month. During the other three weeks, they would discuss the issues by themselves. Mr. and Mrs. Lebo met twice a month for help in reviewing their lives together. At the end of the year, they were able to have family meetings in their own home and talk about each member's personal and family responsibilities. They all agreed that it helped make life in the family more enjoyable.

Jerry Got Lost in the Shuffle

Maxwell J. Schleifer

"Here it is June and we don't know what to do about school plans for our fifteen-year-old son Jerry." Mrs. Quinn, a tall, slender dark-haired woman in her early forties spoke softly. "Jerry is supposed to start the tenth grade at the high school this fall. He has generally been an above-average student. Teachers have always told us that he has more potential than he shows. His discussions in class tend to be more knowledgeable than the work he produces on his school tests. The various achievement tests that they give in school also show he is potentially a superior student.

"In January, we got booklets from the high school to help plan courses. Jerry wanted to take the regular college level courses. He told us that this is what his teachers are recommending and all he feels he can do. My husband and I had wanted him to take the advanced courses, at least in history and French, where he has shown real aptitude in the past. We wanted him to reconsider his decision. So we asked the guidance counselor whether they would wait until the end of the school year before a final decision was made.

"Last week we got a call from Mr. Argovitz, the guidance counselor at the junior high school. He wanted to finalize Jerry's program. He was also concerned about Jerry's school work as well as his mood. He told us Jerry feels that we are expecting too much of him and he doesn't know what to do. He told us that Jerry's school work this spring term was below his usual level. The teachers told Mr. Argovitz that they really weren't worried about what he is learning and that this is not unusual in the last semester for ninth graders. They are more concerned about his participation in school activities.

"Jerry has either been absent or skipped a lot of the preparation for the graduation exercises. Although he has been a reasonably popular youngster, he is not involved in any of the parties or outings. We began to realize this in the last couple of months. When we would ask him what he was doing, he would say that he was staying home and that his friends were going places that he did not want to go. His unhappiness troubles us as much as the school problem.

"This has been a hard year for our family. Jerry has an older brother John who just turned twenty. John has had problems in growing up from the time he was born. When he was one, we were told that he had neuromuscular problems related to cerebral palsy. This has interfered with his learning and his coordination. We've had to struggle every year to make sure that he got the best educational program possible.

"Things have been a lot better ever since the state laws have required special programming for youngsters like John. This has not meant that we have not had to continue to fight for him. He has been in a program at the high school to learn about food services. He has come a long way. He also has some mechanical interests that would make him a reasonable helper at a factory or a repair shop.

"The school people told us there was no more for him to learn at the high school and that they were going to give him a graduation certificate. We felt that he could use more schooling and more training and for several months we made every effort we could to get them to do more. Now we know that while we were so involved in this and some of our other family struggles, we basically ignored Jerry. Right now we're even wondering why we were fighting for John and what we really hoped to get. We realize to a certain extent we are reluctant to face John's trying to enter the job market.

"I've had trouble entering the job market myself. I'd been planning to go back to work for a long time. I hoped as soon as the youngsters could take care of themselves and didn't need me at home I could go back to work full-time. I have been a substitute teacher for the last ten years since Jerry entered kindergarten. But you know how hard it is to find any full-time teaching jobs. I thought I was going to have no trouble because I have taught math and science, but there are no jobs, even in this area in schools. I went to a job counselor myself and I have begun to explore programs in computer sciences which might help retrain me for the job market.

"I know I've been cranky with everybody because of this, and now I wonder what effect this has had on Jerry. My husband is particularly concerned that we do the best for Jerry. He is afraid that if we don't encourage him when he's down that he won't have an opportunity to live up to his own potential. But after the meeting with the counselor we were so unsure that we asked him what he thought would help us and Jerry figure out the best thing. He suggested that we visit you because you've had a lot of experience with youngsters like Jerry and might give us some guidance."

"I feel sad and trapped." Mr. Quinn, a large, heavy-set man in his late forties, spoke. "Jerry is a good kid, and I'm afraid he got lost in the shuffle of other family matters. When I think back on the year I realize how difficult it has been to have a discussion with him. The major area where we have tried to talk to him has been his next year's school plan. And even there I realize that I have had trouble in finding time to discuss anything with him. My mind always was someplace else, generally on John, his older brother, and his problems.

"Jerry is a good son. He doesn't say 'No, I don't want to do this' when we make a suggestion. But he's quiet and I can see the tears in his eyes and that his feelings are hurt. I have found myself confused. On the one hand, I pride myself on being a good listener and at the same time I realize that when Jerry says something I don't agree with, I get upset. In the past year whenever I talk with him about school or sports, he says, 'You think I'm better than I am' or 'You don't think I am trying at all' and that's the end of the discussion.

"We had troubles with his older brother John from the time he was born and we had to make special time for him. We've also made a special effort to make some time for Jerry. And I guess up till this year I would say that we really haven't cheated either boy.

"Sometimes I think we have two families, a family with John and a family with Jerry and we never seem to be able to mix the two. I don't know how we fell into this pattern but that's just the way it's been. I come from a family with a lot of children. I have good relationships with all my brothers. We still call each other when we need help or advice. I do not see any kind of relationship between John and Jerry. That also makes me sad. Maybe you could get some idea from Jerry about what is going on in his head, and I hope you can reassure him that we are not angry. We hope he stops being so disappointed himself. We wish he were happier.

"I realize that John has done very well considering. He's a hardworking kid and he's always been able to hold a summer job of some kind, whether it's been delivering orders for the local grocery or working in the shoe factory. We seem to have been in battles with the school to get a program. But nevertheless I feel that in general the guidance counselors and principals have been as helpful as they could be. This year I probably overreacted when they said they would graduate him. Rather than being pleased with John's progress, I felt angry that he was graduating before he was ready. But he was eager to start a full-time job. I wish I could find a place in the small company that I own but we are a skilled tool and die shop and I don't think John will really be able to work there and I know that's made me sad.

"I don't want Jerry to get less than the best in his education. My wife and I have discussed several ideas which have ranged from having him go to private school where he'd get special attention to going to summer school where they may be able to bring him up to the standard necessary for the advanced courses, to also letting him take the general college level courses. Mr. Argovitz, his guidance counselor, feels that Jerry needs a rest, that even though we may not think so, he's working as hard as he can. Mr. Argovitz is more concerned with the way Jerry feels about himself than about his school work. He feels that if Jerry began to feel better about himself, his school work would improve and I guess that's what's so upsetting and puzzling. I guess up until this year, Jerry's seemed to be a pretty happy-go-lucky kid with a lot of friends although he has been kind of a day-dreamer rather than a worker. How did we all get off the right track and how do we get back on?"

"I am sorry I am so upsetting to my parents." Jerry Quinn, a large, dark-haired fifteen-year-old boy sat on the edge of his chair with tears in his eyes. "They have enough problems without having to worry about me. I know how worried they are about my father's business and my mother's job-hunting problems.

"The last few months in school, I just do not know what happened to me. I seemed to spend all my time daydreaming. I go home every night and promise that I will do the work and yet as soon as I get into my room by myself I have all these thoughts on my mind.

"The teachers were very sympathetic. Maybe that was part of the problem. Maybe they should have been angrier at me. They should have demanded that I do my work. They would only say, 'You're not doing well this term. You got a C on another test. You're not handing in your work.' I would see them after school, and they would tell me to do the best I could.

"I know my father is not sure whether I should be in the high school. He probably told you that. He thought I should be in all the advanced courses.

"I made a visit with my class in January to the high school and it was really very scary. We got a talk from the principal and the head of the guidance department about how hard the high school is. Although I may have done well in junior high the work is going to be twice as tough.

"And then I had fifteen minutes to discuss my plans with the guidance counselor who had been assigned to me. He saw the name and he knew who the family was right away. My brother was at the high school his last four years. He doesn't do very well.

"John and I do not talk to one another. I wish we could. My friends have brothers who tell them about the high school and the teachers and what to do and what not to do. But John and I do not talk to each other much.

"I used to get very upset when my friends would wonder what was wrong with John, but now the kinds of friends I have know him and they know he is a good guy. When I saw him in the lunch room that day, he was sitting all by himself. They call kids like my brother 'dummy' at the high school.

"My parents tell me that things are better than they used to be. But I worry about what is going to happen to John when my parents are not alive anymore. I wish I knew more about what is wrong with him. But my parents never told me. Once I asked and they said that was the way he was born.

"I also know that my parents are well-known for having to fight for John. When I started junior high school, I overheard the teachers talking and saying, 'I hope this kid is better, because I do not want to argue with these parents about what his program should be.' Now I find them wanting to do just that—to fight for my program. This makes me very unhappy.

"I'm not sure what courses I should take or what difference it really makes. Some of my friends know exactly what they want to do or what kinds of jobs they want or colleges they want to go to—I am jealous when I listen to them—they are so sure of themselves. I used to want to be a businessman like my father, but all I hear is how bad business is. I'm not good at math or sciences so I can't get into computers where everybody says there'll be jobs. I don't know what I want.

"Do you know what is wrong with me? Do you know what I should do? Do you know whether I am any good at all?"

DISCUSSION

Jerry Quinn was entering his sophomore year in high school in the fall. His parents were not sure about appropriate curriculum placement for him. They were further puzzled by his increasing school difficulties at the end of the school year.

The guidance counselor suggested that he enter the regular college curriculum courses although it was evident that Jerry had potential for excellent high school work. He felt Jerry's expectations for himself were so high that he undermined his own efforts to succeed. Mr. Argovitz described how Jerry's school work had gone down during the last term and was also worried about Jerry's withdrawal from school activities. Nevertheless, the counselor did not believe that any special or summer work ought to be done.

Mr. Quinn believed that Jerry's potential required that something be done, whether it were repeating another year in the ninth grade or finding some special school system that would help him. The Quinns felt that the energies they had invested in their older son, John, who had cerebral palsy, detracted from their ability to help Jerry.

Jerry felt upset that he had added to his parents' troubles and was as confused as they were about his inability to do better at his school work.

Youngsters who are entering high school are concerned with what they are likely to become. Until then, their own thoughts about their future have been connected with being a member of their own family. At high school, youngsters begin the process of leaving the family and establishing themselves as independent individuals. This question of what they will become is reinforced by the school's implicit or explicit tracking process. Whichever high school curriculums youngsters enter begin to be linked to the kind of career they are likely to have.

Adolescents who successfully move through high school and college generally have the ability to solve and work through the crises of their age by anticipating and thinking about them and taking some preliminary actions.

Jerry's older brother had academic and social difficulties in high school. Jerry observed his parents' anguish about their inability to help him.

Jerry was fearful about his potential for being a successful adult. He was not sure what he wanted to do or what he was capable of becoming. As a result, Jerry was frightened by his view of the future and felt he was not capable of doing anything to help himself deal with the anxiety about taking the next step in growing up; his school work suffered and he withdrew from his friends.

While high school students are struggling with questions of what they will become, the parents are often struggling with the questions of what they have become. Parents' view of themselves is shaped by the success of their careers, marriages, and how well they feel they have brought up their children. Parents who have difficulty in helping one member of the family grow up often have uncertainty about their ability to help their other children.

Mrs. Quinn had been looking forward to returning to a teaching career when her younger son Jerry entered high school. Her concerns about her younger son, and the problems of the older son, as well as the difficulties of entering the job market, undermined her sense of herself as a mother and as a person. It also contributed to her uncertainty about what to do on behalf of her son Jerry.

Mr. Quinn felt that he had failed to provide educational opportunities for his disabled son John and was fearful that he would fail in helping John find a niche in his own life. Not being able to help his son Jerry he experienced as further proof of his shortcomings as a father.

It is not uncommon for families who are having trouble with a child to be unaware of how involved all the other children are in one way or another with the troubles. Although the Quinns had an awareness that the problems of their older son had some influence on Jerry, they were not aware of the extent to which the younger son was concerned, not only with his brother's future, but also with the current anguish and anxiety of his parents.

Jerry was acutely aware of his parents' ups and downs about their struggles for his brother John. Although Jerry was not aware of the particular details, he recognized that their behavior and his brother's behavior influenced their perceptions of him.

Jerry's struggles were associated with challenges appropriate to his age. The challenges that faced his parents with respect to their own lives and to his brother John had an impact on how he felt, as well as how they felt about their ability to understand and help him.

Both parents focused on the family's difficulty in communicating with one another. They accepted this as a problem that needed resolution. They recognized that if they had a clearer idea of what each thought, they all would be in a better position to help each other.

Mr. and Mrs. Quinn and Jerry agreed it would be best if he were to start the fall in a regular college curriculum. They planned to meet with a family therapist every other week to learn how to listen and understand each other. Jerry's ability to concentrate and self-confidence began to improve during the fall. As a result his schoolwork improved considerably. The Quinns all felt that their lives were more interesting at home and were enjoying the time they spent together. In January Jerry was beginning to think about courses that he would take in his junior year. He was actively investigating with his guidance counselor the curriculum options that he would have available. He had some confidence that he could take more advanced courses. He began to do things with his brother on the weekends as well as return to the friendships he had had the previous year.

We Go Our Separate Way, Together but Alone

Maxwell J. Schleifer

"This isn't about my classwork," Donna Greeley, an eighteen-year-old freshman, looked me straight in the eye. "I had a terrible fight with my mother and father at Parents' Weekend. It's the first time I've argued with them in my life. I was very upset when they left to go home. They've had enough trouble without me.

"It's about my ten-year-old sister, Julie. In fact, she's one of the reasons I took your class on Families of Children with Disabilities. I wanted to learn about her and to sort out my feelings about her. As far back as I can remember I worried about Julie and about my mother and father. When Julie was born with brain damage our whole family changed. None of us has been happy since she was born.

"I remember when my mother was still in the hospital with Julie. Everybody was worried. I stayed with my aunt and uncle. I must have been about eight at the time. My father would come from the hospital, he would kiss me hello, and then they would all go into the other room and whisper. I knew something terrible had happened, but I wasn't sure what it was. First, I thought it was my mother, but soon she came home, without Julie—and then I knew it was my sister.

"When Julie finally came home from the hospital, I wasn't allowed to touch her. My grandmother came to live with us for almost a year. My mother stayed in bed most of the time, and my grandmother took care of me. I was never allowed to help with my sister or do anything for her. That was true then, and it's true now.

"I went over all this with my parents last weekend and accused them of keeping me out. They said that all they had ever wanted to do was to protect me from the burdens—the burdens when I grew up. It's the first time they have ever expressed any of this in so many words. There have been times when I was glad to be allowed to go my own way. But there have been other times when I've felt confused and resentful that my parents always went to see Julie without me.

"I told them that I felt I had lost my mother after Julie was born. We used to have such a good time together. We used to be so happy. Mom took me everywhere, to the park, to the museum, to the movies. My father also used to be a lot of fun. We would have great races in the woods behind our house. He taught me how to skate, to play ball. In fact, I became very involved in athletics in high school because of everything my father taught me and did with me when I was a child. He would have loved to teach Julie all these things too. But there was no hope of that, I guess.

"When she got to be a little over three, my parents found a special school for Julie. It's about one hundred miles from where we live. She hadn't developed at all. At three, she was still totally an infant. I saw *The Miracle Worker*, that movie about Helen Keller, and I thought wouldn't it have been wonderful if someone like Annie Sullivan had come to our house to teach Julie how to speak and read and do all the things she taught Helen Keller.

"When I asked my parents last weekend why they finally sent her away, they told me that from the time she was born everybody—the doctors, the nurses, their own parents, my uncle and aunt—felt that she couldn't learn anything at home. After that, my mother went to work to help pay the bills. Since then, it seems we've all been going in different directions.

"Once a month, my parents go to visit Julie for a day, and every summer she comes home for a week. In fact, that's what started the argument. I told my parents that we should have Julie at home the whole summer this year. I think it would do wonders for all of us. We could really be with her and learn about her and discover what she is really like. I said that I would take responsibility for her—taking care of her, keeping her company. I also think we could find things for her to do—programs, activities—in the community. My parents said I was too idealistic, that doing this would be unfair to Julie, that she's happy where she is, they're doing as much as they can, and none of us really knows how to care for her.

"My mother told me something I hadn't known before—that she had tried to find out what she could do. She had even taken some courses given at night at our local community college to learn whatever she could. But nothing she tried convinced her that anything she might do would make a difference. You told us in class there are a lot of new ideas and a lot of new techniques available today for working with brain-damaged children—things that couldn't be done before. My parents don't believe they would work for Julie.

"I was surprised at how little they feel can be done, how little they believe is possible. Both of them have been very involved in a parents' group for brain-damaged children. My father was the one who helped the organization get off the ground. He was the principal fund raiser. He fought for the new legislation. And *he* was even more adamant than my mother about Julie's not coming home.

"I got very upset and told them I thought we were all ashamed of Julie. I know *I* used to be ashamed. I would forget about her when I was in high school. Forget that she even existed. It was because she was home so little, I told myself. When I was growing up I felt there was no need for anybody to know about Julie. But if I got to know someone real well, *then* I could tell them about Julie. But it was always upsetting when any of my friends would see her during those weeks when she was home. Here in college, people naturally ask me about my family. At first, I didn't know whether to tell them I HAD A SISTER WHO IS IN AN INSTITUTION, OR NOT. Then I decided the sooner I began to talk about it, the better I would be able to deal with it. It's been interesting in class to learn that there are three or four other students with similar situations, and that I'm not the only one."

"I'm glad you were willing to see us." Mrs. Greeley, a tiny woman who looked considerably older than her forty years, spoke quietly. "I guess we were all very upset by that argument with Donna over Parents' Weekend. Donna is a very good daughter. I feel badly that she thinks we held out on her so much. I guess my husband and I were more upset than we'd like to admit when Donna said we were ashamed of our own child. I guess she hit a very sore spot.

"We probably should have talked to somebody a long time ago about Julie. Donna's been agitating to bring Julie home this summer. She thinks that she can take responsibility for her. She sees her so seldom she doesn't know about how difficult the day-to-day care of a child like Julie is. Honestly, my husband and I are simply not prepared to have Julie home for any length of time. On the other hand, Al and I disagree about whether at least to have Julie home with us this one summer. It doesn't mean we're committed to having her at home forever, after all! And I think maybe Donna would feel better for knowing that her sister is a real person. Maybe we would all find out something about that.

"My husband and I have never been able, really, to discuss this problem in our lives. I guess it starts with me. To this day, I haven't been able to go back to the obstetrician to ask him about the cause of Julie's brain damage. I always felt there was something problematic in the pregnancy itself. Maybe our genes didn't match. I don't know. Some people say it was probably the delivery, the anesthesia. If I had taken better care of myself, if I had stopped smoking when I was pregnant, maybe Julie wouldn't have been born as she was. 'What if?' Always . . . 'What if?'

"I was overwhelmed by guilt and fear when Julie first came home. I virtually didn't leave the house for six months. My mother took over the care of my family. I spent more time crying in the first six months of Julie's life than most people cry in a lifetime.

"I guess we faced then some of the problems Donna's facing now. *Who* should we tell? *When* should we tell? Should we tell my grandmother? She was very sick. Did she really need to know? Should we tell our relatives in the Midwest? Did *they* really need to know? It was almost as if telling people about Julie would be to admit we had some kind of terrible disease. And I really didn't know what to do with Julie, or how to take care of her. Our pediatrician is a sweet man, but he had no experience with a child such as ours. He was no help. I tried to feed her, to clothe her. I couldn't figure out when to change her, when to feed her. She was just a lump—there in my lap—and there in my throat. It was a terrible time in my life.

"From the moment we brought her home, everybody we talked to said we should put Julie in an institution. At first, I couldn't bear the thought. Julie was my own flesh and blood. How could I put her away? But I wasn't getting anywhere, and nobody offered me any hope. When Julie got to be three, she was still really like a baby. I finally decided that something had to be done. My husband had been urging me to let go of her for some time, and I finally agreed. We found this really very nice school where Julie could stay for her entire life. She has progressed quite a bit, although it's very difficult to understand her when she speaks. She's more like a two- or three-year-old than like a twelve-year-old.

"I know there are new programs today in which she might be doing even better. I know that some young mothers are keeping their disabled children at home. They have special people come in to help them teach the baby how to eat and how to sit and how to crawl—all the little things that I didn't know how to do for Julie. My husband and I have been very active in parents' organizations for brain-damaged children in our town and in our state. We've advocated and raised money to provide for some of these new programs. It's ironic that we're the very ones who are reluctant to find out whether any of these programs would make a difference for *us*. I think it's time for us to think about these things, and incidentally, now that Donna's away in college, to figure out what kind of a life we want to lead."

Mr. Greeley, a slight, gray-haired man in his early fifties, spoke quickly. He was tense and there were tears in his eyes. "I was very surprised at how upset and angry Donna was. We'd always gotten along so well together. I've always assumed that we were doing the best we could do, and that we all were in agreement on what we were doing—even though, I'll admit, we've never really discussed our concerns about Julie with each other.

"It's time that Marie and I did something about our marriage. Ever since Julie was born we haven't had much of a relationship. Our focus is on our children; we work together for them. Marie has gone to work to help pay for the costs of Julie's school. We also are very committed to Donna. But we don't have any fun together. Maybe people don't think of me as a fun person, and I don't believe life is a bowl of cherries, but something is missing, and we are aware of it now that Donna's away at school.

"Those first six months when my wife came home with Julie she was very depressed, and my mother-in-law moved in. I'm sorry we did it that way. It would have been better to hire a competent stranger. With my mother-in-law around, I didn't have a chance to talk about all this with Marie, to get things off my chest. I think I always felt she was accusing me, as if it were my fault. My wife has been so afraid of having another child it has destroyed our sex life. We've hedged around the topic of contraception, I've even toyed with the idea of sterilization, but truthfully, this part of our life is over. We go our separate ways, together but alone.

"There *are* good new programs today. I'm aware of them. It would have been helpful if there had been more of this kind of information twelve years ago, when Julie was born. About the causes of brain damage, for example— what is hereditary and what is not. With my wife, I've helped start a lot of these programs. We've tried to support whatever we could. But I know it's a battle every step of the way. That's what you people in the colleges don't understand. You write about it in the textbooks as if it's easy. I see the publicity on television. I read the books. I go to the meetings. But I don't think we've made many grand slam successes. It's an uphill battle.

"I do know that Julie has been on Donna's mind a lot more since she went away to college. My wife told me she and Donna had a talk about sex and marriage, and that one of Donna's questions was about her chances of having a child like Julie. Donna doesn't realize how hard it would be to have Julie at home for the whole summer. You know, it's like when we got our dog, Muffin. Donna said she would take care of him, but you know who wound up doing the walking and the training and the cleaning. I know Julie's not an animal, but . . . it's so easy for kids to make promises and commitments without knowing whether they can keep them. I wish we had taken Donna into our confidence more when she was growing up, and I wish we could make up for it now."

DISCUSSION

Donna Greeley, a college freshman, came to see me after the Monday meeting of our class on Families of Children with Disabilities. During Parents' Weekend she had had an argument with her parents about the care and the fate of her twelve-year-old sister, Julie. She had insisted that Julie come home for the whole summer this year. Julie had been placed in a residential school for severely disabled children when she was three. Donna only saw her during a one-week vacation at home each summer. Donna accused her parents of living in the nineteenth century. She insisted that it was their shame about Julie that kept them from bringing Julie home and from taking advantage of the opportunities now available for children like her. Donna took action because of the things she had been learning in class. She asked whether I would be willing to talk to her parents.

The Greeleys were eager to discuss their quarrel with their daughter. They were upset and surprised by the intensity of her feelings. She had always been a cheerful, cooperative youngster, and had never challenged their views or actions in any way. They wondered whether something else was disturbing her, whether there were any problems in school or in her life that they should be aware of. We agreed that there was a lot to talk about, and decided to meet together several times before deciding on a course of action.

Both the Greeleys were skeptical about whether the attitudes of society toward individuals with disabilities or toward their families have really changed in the past few years. They were even less confident of the adequacy of the new programs. They agreed that their life "had not been the same" after Julie's birth, that the joy had gone out of their life together. Both parents had a considerable emotional investment in their elder daughter, Donna, and in her success.

Mrs. Greeley re-lived the impact of the experience of having Julie. She recalled her severe depression during those first six months of Julie's life. She described what she had tried, and how consistently she had failed. The Greeleys both emphasized the lack of support they found in their families, among their friends, and from professionals, as well as the generally negative, hopeless attitude toward disabilities in society at large. Mr. Greeley was particularly bitter about the professionals they'd met up with around Julie's birth. He felt entirely excluded from their discussions. He had never been able to discuss with anyone the changes in his and his wife's relationship—the evaporation of their sex life and pleasure in each other. He had taken great pride in Donna, and in many ways had used her as a "substitute" for his wife. His skeptical attitude toward the possibility of change was influenced by his concern that he was losing his daughter to "these new ideas."

Over the years, the Greeleys had united and collaborated in their effort to provide more and better services for children with brain damage. Although they began this work in an effort to find the best facility for their own daughter, they became advocates for the improvement of services to all youngsters with disabilities. Deep down, however, they remained so bound up in their own personal struggle to come to terms with their decision about Julie that their ambivalence pervaded their approach to the question of whether social attitudes and programs had shifted. In addition, their experience with professionals made them reluctant to try some of the new programs close to home.

The Greeleys' skepticism about new programs was part of their total experience. The confusion and conflict in society-at-large about people with disabilities are reflected in the limited opportunities—socially, educationally, and vocationally—that were available in the past for youngsters born with disabilities. Conditions have changed in the 1970s, and we can expect in the 1980s that there will be more opportunities than ever. The Greeleys questioned the depth of these attitudinal changes, and whether they would result in programs that would be helpful to their own child.

Donna was in the midst of "pulling up roots," having just made her first major move away from her family. She was living at school, having to confront the different attitudes and value systems of the faculty members and other adults around her as well as those of other young people, students coming from all over the state. She was struggling with the task of sorting out which ideas were her own, which were her parents', and which were those of her new friends. The pressures of dating, sex, and marriage also loomed in her life for the first time. Her lack of direct knowledge and experience of her sister, together with the absence of open discussion in the family about Julie, left Donna with few resources as she moved into that time when she would be making decisions about her own life. In the class on Families of Disabled Children, she discovered other young people with brothers or sisters with problems similar to Julie's. She found herself discussing out loud for the first time issues that had been on her mind for a long time. In this context of shared concern, interest, information, and support for her ideas, Donna found herself wanting to "open things up" with her parents. The intensity of the argument with her parents was a reflection of her own struggles.

We all view changes within the context of our individual life experiences. This is as true for professionals as it is for parents. Early experiences in our careers as parents or professionals shape the way we view new experiences. Both parents and professionals who have been defeated in their efforts to help particular youngsters thrive and grow often view new programs with doubt and skepticism. At the time the Greeleys' daughter was born, neither parents nor professionals had had much "experience of success" at their common disposal, and their were few practical (or inner, emotional) resources for trying out new ideas. As in the Greeleys' situation, professionals generally supported programs that removed disabled children from their families and placed them in institutions.

By contrast, new programs tend to be exciting to the young—professionals and laypersons alike. Not having had many negative and defeating experiences, young people tend to look optimistically at new possibilities. Whether they have been mandated by law or shaped by the new willingness of the community, these new programs have provided us all with a wide range of experience and expertise that did not exist before. These experiences have allowed us to refine old programs and develop new ones. The Greeleys are right, of course, that optimistic attitudes, in and of themselves, do not change life. However, when we are struggling with our own feelings, the uncertainty and hesitation of others around us make it difficult to sort out which problems belong to us and which belong to others.

After meeting with Mr. and Mrs. Greeley a few times, Donna, her parents and I convened a meeting together to discuss the issues that had come up in our individual conversations. Donna was able to discuss calmly with her parents her concerns about Julie and her sense that these concerns were mutual. She listened to them, in turn, and tried to understand their reluctance to see her involved with her sister. She shared some of her fantasies of Julie that had mushroomed because of her lack of involvement and contact with her "real sister." Even as she confided in them, she gently but straightforwardly criticized their parenting where Julie was concerned. The Greeleys agreed to search the community for ways of making it possible for Julie to live at home this summer. Mrs. Greeley felt that she and her husband had to create a new life together, free of the burdens and misunderstandings of the past. She was eager to do some digging into her own past. Mr. Greeley was much more skeptical of looking into the future, or the past. Mrs. Greeley decided to seek some counseling for herself, even if her husband wasn't willing to do so at this time. Mr. Greeley took responsibility for the work of looking for programs and opportunities for Julie in the community.

I'm Not Going to Be John's Baby Sitter Forever

Maxwell J. Schleifer

"I am glad you were able to see us so quickly," Mrs. Holmes, a short, light-haired woman in her early fifties spoke sadly. "Last week my husband and I discovered we had a family problem. We hadn't realized it existed until our twenty-five-year-old son Jimmy exploded at a meeting we were having with him and our daughter Julia, who is twenty-three. We were discussing what we were planning to do about our will.

"We had not included our youngest son John, who is sixteen and has a developmental disability. We had been asked by our lawyer, Mr. Simmons, to update our will. Mr. Simmons suggested we should do it now because of the new tax laws and the new federally funded programs available for community living and rehabilitation. He thought we ought to make sure we have adequately provided for Johnny.

"We spent a lot of time on what I guess you would call the legal details of our lives. We want to make sure that we provide the maximum amount of income for John in such a way that it won't interfere with his eligibility for the various government programs. Mr. Simmons did what he usually does and discussed with us who should be the major trustee or executor of the will. We discussed the importance of choosing someone who knew a lot about the management of money, somebody who would be interested in John, someone who would understand our interests in managing money, and someone who would be able to change with the times and make adjustments as programs might change and as Johnny might change. We then had to consider what role family members might play as opposed to people like our lawyer, the current executor of our will.

"My husband Ken and I thought we ought to talk with Jimmy and Julia to share the thoughts we had. We wanted to know how they felt about the plans and their thoughts about Johnny before we finalized any plan with Mr. Simmons.

"Out of the blue, Jimmy started shouting that he was not going to be his brother's baby sitter for the rest of his life. He obviously was angry and said that maybe he shouldn't see us for the next several months so that we could all sort things out. He stormed out of the house and went back to his apartment. He has lived in his own apartment since he started law school, but has kept in touch constantly and usually visits sometime each weekend. I burst into tears as soon as he left.

"Although we always had to pay attention to John's special needs for help and support, I thought that we had always been fair about family matters. Our kids have always been great at helping out. They were always willing to walk that extra mile when my husband or I were too tired or too busy to attend to some of John's activities.

"Julia has been very helpful and supportive, but Jimmy always seemed to have an extra special place in his heart for John and did special things for him. I don't think we forced any of this on him. I don't think we made him do it. But from the time John came home from the hospital, Jimmy has been very attentive to John's needs as well as mine.

"When Jimmy was in elementary school, the first thing he did when he came home was to check on John. He always saw how John was doing before he went out to play with his own friends. Jimmy got very involved with the Special Olympics when John was nine years old. He has continued to work not only with John, but with the various community recreation programs that John has been involved with. In the winter, it's basketball; in the spring, it's softball; and in the summer, they enjoy swimming. Jimmy has always been exceptionally proud of his brother and John worships the ground Jimmy walks on.

"When Jimmy shouted at us, I felt sick to my stomach. I still don't know how to explain his behavior to anybody. I wasn't exactly sure what we would say to John. How would I tell him Jimmy wasn't going to be coming around?

"When Jim left, we asked Julia if we made her feel the same way. Julia is a very mature twenty-three-year-old. Ever since she was fifteen we could always trust her to take responsibility for her own life. She shopped for her own clothes, made her own college plans and last month she took an apartment with two friends from college. Her roommates all have jobs teaching school. She told us she didn't understand what was bugging Jim and she admitted feeling very responsible for John even though we never discussed it. She thought Jimmy has been very cranky since he broke up with his girlfriend, but he loves us all.

"At the end of last week, Jimmy called to apologize. Ken and I told Jimmy that an apology wasn't as important as understanding his tensions so that we could work out a solution that would help all of us. I had been so upset that I had gone to our family doctor for sleeping pills. Our family doctor recommended that we see a family counselor and he gave us your name. I don't know what sense you can make of all this, I can only say that I am surprised and a little scared."

"I am not sure that we should make more of this situation than it is," Ken Holmes, a short, slender man in his late fifties spoke quickly. "I am sure it was just the heat of the moment. I don't know what else was happening in Jimmy's life at the time, but I can't believe he really feels we've made him into a life-long baby sitter.

"At the same time, I guess without discussing them, we do have expectations or beliefs about our kids. We hope they will remain involved with one another as long as they're alive. We have assumed that our kids would look after Johnny when we were gone. That's the way it's been with our own families. We're there to share the good times and help with the bad times. We've been very pleased about how well we've all gotten along. It hasn't always been a very good situation for any of us, but I think that if you took a look at us from a distance, you would say we're good people, we've got good kids and we've got a good family.

"We've tried to make sure that each child's needs have been considered. We've tried to explain to Jimmy and Julia the questions we have about the management of funds. Jimmy is in his second year of law school. Hopefully, he will finish next year and begin a career of his own. Julia has finished college. She has taken a job as a teacher while she figures out what she wants to do with the rest of her life. Jimmy and Julia worked to supplement the money we gave them for college and they are also stuck with some hefty college loans.

"We certainly are more optimistic about John's future than we were when he was born. He has been involved with excellent school and recreational programs. Right now, John is in a school program that is teaching him how to work. As part of a job training program, he is working in the kitchen at the local hospital two hours a day. I think he is an awfully nice kid. With a little luck and back-up, he should be able to have some kind of a job with a fast food chain or a hospital. Who can tell what might happen!

"We've had some great times together. We have not asked Julia and Jimmy to be John's parents. But at my age, when you have to write a will, you realize that you won't be able to take care of things forever. Maybe we should not expect Julia and Jimmy to remain involved with John their whole life. Who knows where they will live and whether life will bring them good or bad fortune.

"Jean and I have spent so much time trying to help all our children, we have sometimes forgotten ourselves. We have been so focussed on dealing with all the problems of today, we have not really considered the future, not only for our kids, but for ourselves. Our lawyer's insistence that we update our will has forced us to do planning we have put off for far too long. But doing it scares me."

"I'm embarrassed by the problems that I've created for everybody," Jimmy, a tall red-headed young man in his early twenties glancing at his parents spoke quickly. "I don't know what got into me. I love my brother John, maybe that's part of the problem. When I was growing up it was always difficult for me to see myself apart from my family. It was almost as if I thought my parents would live forever. I also always saw myself helping John and taking care of him.

"But I realize that John is sixteen years old now. Somehow, in my dreams, it was almost as if he would always be about eight or nine. But he started growing up and becoming an adult. I don't know what came over me when I started to complain about having responsibility for him. Actually, he is much more independent and capable of caring for himself than any of us dreamed of.

"There's a lot of things going on in my own life, too. It's a surprise and sort of upsetting when your mother and father talk about their will. It's hard to plan for the future and think about them dying. Their intentions were very good. Obviously, they wanted to tell me and my sister what they wanted to do, and how they wanted to do it. They wanted to talk about how Julie and I would be involved with my brother. When I look at it, and as I talk to my friends and my sister, they really tried to prepare us all for what will happen to us. Sooner or later, parents die.

"This is a bad time for me now. I am trying to figure out what I want to do and where I want to go. My friends at law school are all getting ready for job interviews and they are all discussing where they want to go and where the best opportunities are. I am ashamed to say I still don't know what to do. And I feel paralyzed.

"When I started college, I assumed that I would stay in the city that I'm living in right now. But I want to give myself a chance to see the rest of the country, visit other places. I've had friends, both in college and in law school, from the west coast, the southwest and the midwest. I say to myself sometimes, life is much too short to lock yourself into one place. But then I say, if I move, what will it mean to John, what will happen to my relationship with Julia. My relatives live near us and I get to see my aunts, uncles and cousins all the time. It's been great! I begin to say to myself, what if I really do move away, where will the family be? I think that's what I find upsetting.

"Lately, I've been thinking my parents are to blame for making me stay in this area. Then I start blaming it on my brother. Then I think about what will happen to me. I realize I'm becoming independent of my whole family, my parents as well as Julia and John. What kind of a life does that leave me? I find it very confusing.

"We really have been a great family. I think anybody who knows us would agree. We've done things that we've had to do and we've taken care of each other when we've had to. My parents have been very good to us. I am still troubled and confused as to why I shouted at my parents and I don't want it to happen again."

DISCUSSION

Mr. and Mrs. Holmes had begun a discussion of their will with their oldest son and daughter. Part of the will focused on John, their youngest son, who has a developmental disability. The Holmeses were upset when their oldest son James angrily denounced what he considered their expectation—that he spend his life taking care of his brother. The Holmeses felt it was important to be able to review their relationship with their son with a professional. Mr. and Mrs. Holmes, along with James, agreed that they have had a hard-working, close-knit family relationship. They had provided a constructive life environment for all of their children including their son with a developmental disability. All of them struggled to understand what could have precipitated such a crisis.

Families change during the course of their lifetime, beginning with marriage, to the birth of their first child and continuing through the separation of their last child from the family structure. Families have developmental tasks that must be mastered and met during this long period of time. These challenges parallel the tasks that individual members have to face themselves.

Discussion and preparation of a will marks, both for parents and children, the ending of the child-rearing phase of family life. Parents often see the independence and life of their children as a measure of the success of their own lives. They have an opportunity to do more together as they live life without children. They have to decide how they will deal with the last phase of their lives. The children are reminded of their own developmental status as adults. They also have to review the changing pattern of relationships within the family—the moving from more dependent status to independence of their own.

Each family has its own style of dealing with these issues. Families that are close knit are often surprised to find how difficult the changing status can be. They assume that they have gotten along well for so many years that changes and shifts of status within the family will be smooth. Changing roles require specific definitions. Children have to be able to define, in their own terms, their new relationships with their parents and their own needs in order to be independent. In families where people do not get along, everybody looks forward to when people can be independent of each other.

In changing, people have to give up the expectations of family members and the view of themselves that belongs to earlier years. James, like many young adults, had to give up the picture of nobody ever growing older—the picture of his relationship to his brother that he described. Sometimes, youngsters like Jim find it easier to insist that their parents want to keep them dependent rather than admit their own doubts about the independence.

Families that are close knit are often surprised at the difficulty children have leaving home when they are young adults. Many, like Jim, leave in anger. It is often more difficult for people to discuss the positive aspects of their relationship than the negative. The negative is out in the open and demands a resolution. It is much more difficult for people to talk about their concerns and care for each other.

The Holmes family knew they cared for one another. They had never discussed what this would mean and how it would be reflected in this stage of their family life. They began to make their expectations of each other explicit. They were able to accept the unpredictability of their lives in the future. They could begin to examine the different jobs that would have to be done to maximize John's future opportunities for a good life. Each member of the family began to distinguish between John's financial, social and emotional needs and their own.

Mr. and Mrs. Holmes selected an executor of their will who was an expert in the management of funds. At the suggestion of their lawyer, they selected a younger member of the firm because he would be available for a long period of John's life. Jim, Julia and John had a series of meetings with the executor so they could get to know and understand each other. The will was written so that either Jim or Julia could take more responsibility for John's portion of the future estate if it became necessary.

PART V

Young Siblings

"Family Album" became a regular feature in *Exceptional Parent* in order to give children an opportunity to share their views of the world. In this section, ten girls and boys, all twelve years of age or younger, describe their relationships with their siblings who are disabled. As in Part IV, all but one of these young authors is an older sibling of a child with a disability.

Sometimes adults are uncertain about how much children understand about the life of their family. In these short articles, the girls and boys make clear that they have learned about their sibling's disability and are aware of the similarities and differences between themselves and their siblings. They have learned from their interactions with their siblings, as well as from their parents, and they want to be helpful and are interested in educating others.

It is gratifying to read the words of these youngsters because it is clear that they have learned from their parents, as well as their siblings, that it is acceptable to talk openly about relationships and feelings. Their comfort in applying the lessons of this book is reassuring evidence of the changing climate of community life for children with disabilities, their siblings, and their parents.

Lydia and Trevor

Lydia Mills

Hi! My name is Lydia and I am eight years old. I have a brother and his name is Trevor. He is special because he is retarded. And I am special too because I am cross-eyed sometimes.

I am glad that I have a brother because we play together. We play games. And, Trevor's favorite thing is cars and we say prayers together at dinner-time. My family loves him.

Nathan and Timmy

Nathan Long

Hi! My name is Nathan. I am six years old and will be starting first grade. I have a little brother, Timmy, who is disabled, but we call him a "special" boy. I like that name better. He is three years old and was born with part of his brain missing. He has a blue wheelchair. I like to push him around in it. He can't walk or do much, but he can make some noises. Sometimes, he says, "Na." I think he means to say "Nathan."

I took him to school. One kid asked me why he is like that. I told them that all people are different and that he is kind of like Rudolph the red-nosed reindeer. He was different too, but special. Timmy liked that I took him for show-and-tell. I like to play with Timmy, he likes music. I like him for a brother and is special to me. I love him very, very much.

Randy and Robert

Robert Rutland-Brown

I have a brother, Randy. He just turned five. My name is Robert. Randy is handicapped, which makes me sad. We still do fun things together. We share a room. Whenever he wakes up, he says "Dirt, up!" (Randy can't pronounce Robert so he calls me "Dirt.")

Randy can only see a little bit. Randy has trouble moving his right hand. He can't walk yet, so he crawls around on the floor. He has a pair of special shoes that might help him learn to walk.

Randy and I play "mommy and baby" together. Whoever is the mommy takes care of the baby, changes his diaper, gives him a drink, and sometimes reads him a book. Another game we play is called the taste game. I give him different kinds of food. If he knows what it is he says the name of the food. If he doesn't know the name of the food, or doesn't like it, he says "Yuck."

Randy has a battery operated car he can drive around in the front yard. The only problem is that he might go in the street or run over the neighbors' plants, so I stay out there and keep an eye on Randy. Randy's a great swimmer. He can swim the width of the pool without a breath. But I'm always scared that he might not know where he is or get tired and drown, so I stay close to him.

I'm sad that Randy's handicapped, but I know there's nothing I can do about it. My friends think Randy's special because other little sisters and brothers are ordinary sisters or brothers. Randy will always be special to me.

My Little Brother

Crystal Ravizza

Hi! My name is Crystal, I am ten years old. I have a story to tell you about my little brother Michael. He first came to live with my family in October of 1985. He was 1-1/2 years old. When the social worker brought him to our house he looked different to me. She said that Michael is handicapped. He was not a happy boy because he did not have a family. But we love Mikey very much and that makes him happy. Michael lived with us for one year, but we had to move to California. So Michael had to live with a new foster mom. Then my mom and my big sister went to Connecticut on an airplane to bring Mikey to California to live with us. In August 1987 our family adopted Mikey. His new name is Michael Anthony Ravizza. On January 20, 1989 Michael turned 5 years old. He makes lots of happy sounds and laughs and smiles when he is happy. Michael likes to give us hugs and loves kisses too. He likes to listen to his music and he is learning to play with special toys. Michael is handicapped because he needs a shunt to drain the fluid from his brain, he is blind and is fed by a special tube in his stomach. But that is OK with me. I love my brother very much because he is my brother and he makes me happy!

Andrew

Jill Kasper

Andrew is a disabled child. He is also my brother. Andrew has hydrocephalus. Hydrocephalus is water-on-the-brain. At two weeks old, doctors had to put a shunt in to relieve the pressure. Otherwise, his head would have continued to grow until it burst. A shunt is a tube running from the brain to the abdominal cavity. Sometime he will have to have his shunt replaced, because he will outgrow his old one.

He also has epilepsy as a result of having the shunt. That means he has seizures. They started when he was four years old. A seizure is something you have when the electricity in your brain does not run smoothly. There are many different kinds of seizures. Some seizures make you pass out, fall down, and jerk your arms and legs. Others make you confused and stare into space. My brother loses consciousness and jerks the entire right side of his body. His seizure is called a partial Jacksonian. Most people think that seizures last only a few minutes, but they are wrong. They can last very long. My brother had one that lasted two hours. His seizures are very serious. He always has to go to the hospital by ambulance and get special medicine to come out of it.

Seizures usually happen when medicine levels are too low. My brother has to go have bloodwork done at least once every month, to make sure his medicine levels are right. When the levels are off, he goes more often. My brother takes two kinds off medicine. They are called Tegretol and Depakene. He is learning to swallow pills called Depakote which will work better than the Depakene syrup. He does not like to take his medicine now.

School is difficult for Andrew. Between the medicine he takes and the brain damage he has, he will have to work very hard.

Epilepsy means you might never drive a car, have a job, or even get insurance. Some people don't want to have anything to do with epileptics. So, if you meet people with epilepsy or any other handicap, be nice to them, and don't laugh at them if they can't do something! They need friends too.

Melon

Jessica Crawford

Melon is the nickname of my three-year-old sister Jamilyn. She was born with a birth defect called spina bifida. She also has hydrocephalus and Chiari syndrome. When she was born her spine was open and she had surgery to close it. A week later she had another surgery to implant a shunt to relieve water pressure on her brain.

Since then, she has had many more surgeries and hospitalizations for infections. Usually our whole family stays with her in the hospital or close by at the Ronald McDonald House.

Melon needs lots of special care. I try to help as much as I can. Her bladder doesn't work that well, so she has to be catheterized every three hours. My mom taught me how to do this when Melon was about eight months old. I also help with her physical, speech and occupational therapy.

Melon is learning to walk with a walker, but for most activities away from home she uses a wheelchair. I have two other sisters; one is eight years old and one three months old. It takes a lot of effort for her to do things, so our whole family is really excited when she makes progress. I'm really glad she's my sister, so when you see someone with a physical or mental disability, SMILE—they have feelings too.

A Story about Zoe

Simone Chess

My sister Zoe is autistic. That means her brain doesn't work the same way most people's brains work. She can't talk at all, and she doesn't seem to understand words. Zoe is on medicine that is supposed to help her brain. She used to take Depakene, a syrupy and probably disgusting thing. But now she is on Depakote. To you this is probably very boring, but let me say that by simply changing her medicine from syrup to pills she did the impossible. She swallowed a pill! I, an eight-year-old, can't swallow a pill, yet she, a handicapped four-year-old, can!

You must think that I wish she was normal. Obviously, I do. Sometimes she is a big pain. But she has her good points. I LOVE to sing to her in the car. She loves and cares about my family. She loves my mom and dad. She loves me, she loves my brother and she loves my younger sister, too.

Zoe has taught me many things. She has taught me that no matter how different people seem to be, they all have feelings. She has taught me to be brave. But most importantly, she has taught me that if you hope hard enough, almost anything can come true and I should never EVER give up on her.

I know that many, MANY people out there are working hard to help people like Zoe, including my mother and father. I will too. After all, Zoe is like a scrambled word. She has all the letters, but they're in the wrong order. I am going to try my very best to unscramble that word and find the real Zoe underneath that terrible mask.

My Brother

Gena Appleby

My brother is retarded. He is eight years old. All he watches on TV is our home videos. He probably memorized all of them. He'll never go anywhere without his plastic horns. If he has a hammer or anything long, he'll bang it on furniture or our bath tub. I always have my room door closed or else he will get into all my stuff.

After awhile you understand what he's trying to say. He puts his hands to his mouth when he's hungry.

A lot of times in the summer he runs around the neighborhood and then my mom has to go find him. Our neighborhood is real small, so it's not dangerous.

Our dog chews up his toys and he plays with the dog's toys. He loves Mickey Mouse. Don't ask why! By the way, his name is Collin.

It's not always easy taking care of a retarded brother, but I love him.

My Sister Whitney

Lindsey Kohnert

My sister Whitney is three years old. When she was six months old we noticed she wasn't doing anything. We went to lots of doctors to see what she had. Today people still can't tell what she has. She wears braces on her legs. She can't walk or talk but she's trying. Hopefully someday people can tell what she has. Hopefully that day will come soon.

My Brother John is Handicapped

Summer Hargreaves

My brother John is handicapped. John uses a light talker to speak to you. John uses a wheelchair to get around in. John is very smart. John is five years old. John's in kindergarten in a regular classroom. John's teacher's name is Mrs. Pifer. John has games on his light talker. John can even play the computer. John has a head switch.

When John sees the picture he wants he hits the switch. John has physical therapy almost every day. John is just like you, but John is handicapped. John has a disease, but he can't spread it. It's a handicapped disease, but John's not sick. John was born that way. John has "Cowabunga, Dude!" on his light talker. John is nice, but sometimes by accident John pulls my hair when he is spastic. John loves me very much and I love him, too. John's the best brother I ever had!

Conclusion

We called this book *It Isn't Fair!* because as they confront the day to day challenges of parenting a child with a disability and as their growing children repeatedly protest their perceptions of parental unfairness, parents may wonder about the relative fairness of their lives. We also chose the title because the theme of fairness appears in various forms in so many of the articles—whether written by parents, siblings, or professionals.

Each of the authors who contributed to this book—adult siblings and young siblings, parents and professionals—are helping to light the way for other siblings, parents, and professionals. They have shown us that while the relationships between sisters and brothers may be complicated, the fact that one sibling has a disability does not necessarily make the sibling relationship problematic.

All parents worry about the relationships among their children and how these relationships may affect each child in the years to come. They are eager to know the experiences of others that might be applicable.

When we first published *Exceptional Parent* magazine in 1971, there was very little parenting information for parents of children with disabilities to share—about sibling relationships, or anything else. Thankfully, much has changed. In today's climate of educational, vocational, social, and community changes for the better, in the lives of children with disabilities and their parents, the wisdom of the contributors to this book can be applied with increasing optimism and resolve as we seek continued improvement in the lives of all children and families.

Resources

ORGANIZATIONS

The Sibling Information Network

The Sibling Information Network is an organization for families and professionals who are interested in the welfare of individuals with disabilities and their families, specifically siblings.

Made up of approximately 1,800 members, the network provides a common information base, serving as a clearinghouse for research and other professional activities related to siblings of children with disabilities.

The network distributes a quarterly *Newsletter*, available free to members. Other available resources include bibliographies of children's literature and relevant journal articles, a listing of audiovisual materials, and suggestions on how to start a sibling group.

For information contact Sibling Information Network, The University of Connecticut, A. J. Pappanikou Center, 991 Main Street, East Hartford, CT 06108, (203)282-7050.

The Sibling Support Project

The Sibling Support Project addresses the specific concerns associated with brothers and sisters of children with special needs. The issues the project covers include isolation, caregiving responsibilities, guilt, pressure to achieve, and questions about the siblings' future. The project strives to increase the number of peer support programs throughout the United States.

Such programs are based on the Sibling Support Project's "Sibshop Model." Sibshops seek to elicit coping strategies, foster mutual support, and encourage self-expression.

The project provides the training, demonstration, and technical assistance to agencies wishing to add a program for brothers and sisters. Staff members also work to increase awareness of sibling issues through presentations to national and regional audiences.

For information contact the Sibling Support Project at Children's Hospital and Medical Center, 4800 Sand Point Way N.E., Seattle, WA 98105, (206)368-4911.

BOOKLET

Morgan, F. *The Pittsburgh Sibling Handbook*. Pittsburgh: The Easter Seal Society of Allegheny County, 1992. This informative booklet is available at a cost of $3.50 plus $1.50 for shipping and handling from: The Sibling Support Project, Easter Seal Society of Allegheny County, 632 Fort Duquesne Blvd., Pittsburgh, PA 15222.

BOOKS

Grossman, F. K. *Brothers and Sisters of Retarded Children*. Syracuse, NY: Syracuse University Press, 1972.

Meyer, D., Vadasy, P. & Fewell, R. R. *Living With a Brother or Sister With Special Needs*. Seattle: University of Washington Press, 1985.

Powell, T. & Ogle, P. *Brothers and Sisters: A Special Part of Exceptional Families*. Baltimore: Paul Brookes, 1985.

Powell, T. & Gallagher, P. A. *Brothers and Sisters: A Special Part of Exceptional Families. Second Edition*. Baltimore: Paul Brookes, 1992.

Seligman, M. & Darling, R. B. *Ordinary Families, Special Children: A Systems Approach to Childhood Disability*. New York: Guilford Press, 1989. (*See* Chapter 5, "Effects on Siblings.")

Index

About the Editors

STANLEY D. KLEIN is Co-Founder and Publisher of *Exceptional Parent* magazine, a Professor of Psychology at the New England College of Optometry, and a Research Associate in Medicine (General Pediatrics) at Children's Hospital in Boston. He is the author of *Psychological Testing of Children*: *A Consumer's Guide* (1977) and co-editor (with Maxwell Schleifer) of *The Disabled Child and the Family* (1985).

MAXWELL J. SCHLEIFER is Co-Founder and Publisher of *Exceptional Parent* magazine, a Professor of Psychology at the University of Massachusetts, Boston, and a Visiting Professor at the Smith College School of Social Work. He is co-editor (with Stanley Klein) of *The Disabled Child and the Family* (1985).